Perfect D...

STOCKHOLM

Travel with **Insider Tips**

MARCO POLO

Contents

 TOP 10   4

That Stockholm Feeling   6

For chapters: See inside front cover

Not to be missed!
Our TOP 10 hits – from the absolute No. 1 to No. 10 –
help you plan your tour of the most important sights.

⭐ **ROYAL PALACE** ➤ 80
One of the largest palaces in the world. Located in the city centre, the royal apartments and treasury attract many visitors. The changing of the guard is a dashing exercise in military precision.

⭐ **VASA MUSEUM** ➤ 104
The *Vasa* battleship that sank on its maiden voyage sat at the bottom of the sea for 333 years. Today it can be admired in its own museum.

⭐ **SKANSEN** ➤ 109
In the Skansen Open-Air Museum, you can wander through Sweden and around 140 historic buildings, and even look round a whole city district.

⭐ **CITY HALL** ➤ 50
Stockholm's landmark. The Golden Hall is famous for its enormous mosaics, and there is a lovely view from the tower over the entire city.

⭐ **STORTORGET** ➤ 85
Old merchant houses, cosy little cafés and the Nobel Museum surround the Stortorget (photo). It is a very special public square, although there have been dark tales in its history, too. The Stockholm Bloodbath took place here in 1520.

⭐ **ABBA THE MUSEUM** ➤ 112
Agnatha, Björn, Benny and Anni-Frid are still standing in the spotlight in this museum. It is not only fans that are delighted by the multimedia exhibition.

⭐ **SOFO & MEDBORGARPLATSEN** ➤ 136
A relaxed night out or serious partying – both are possible in the district to the south of Fokungagatan. During the day, the district's exciting shops and boutiques pull in the crowds.

⭐ **HAGA PARK** ➤ 54
This is a good area to live. Haga Palace in the park of the same name is the home of the Crown Princess Victoria and Prince Daniel. It is nestled in a magnificent landscape park laid out in the English style.

⭐ **RIDDARHOLMEN CHURCH** ➤ 87
A total of 17 kings have found their final resting place in the burial church of the Swedish Royal Family.

⭐ **WALDEMARSUDDE** ➤ 115
In this dream location on Djurgården, Prince Eugen had a representative villa built in 1903–05 which is now home to one of the most beautiful museums in Stockholm.

THAT
STOCKHOLM

Find out what makes the city tick, experience its unique flair – just like the Stockholmers themselves.

TACK, TACK AND TACK AGAIN

Swedish courtesy is legendary. They thank you for everything, absolutely everything. A Swede would never think of accepting a service without expressing a friendly *tack*. The person addressed expresses his gratitude for the thanks with "*tack, tack*". And if someone wants to be particularly affable, then he says, "*tack, tack, tack*" to the person who has just thanked him. Even if this seems a little excessive, just play along, it pays to be courteous in Sweden. But beware: Don't interpret this friendliness as an invitation for excessive bonhomie. Swedes appreciate a certain amount of restraint.

THE CITY FROM ABOVE

Stockholm boasts a unique location between Lake Mälar and the Baltic Sea. That is why it is so rewarding to look out across the city. There are countless ways to do that. The most well-known option is the view from the City Hall Tower (► 50), but there is also a beautiful view of the Old Town from Fjällgata street

(► 138) or Monteliusvägen path (► 148) in the Södermalm district. And then there is also the SkyView from the roof of the Ericsson Globe (► 144) and the viewing platform of the radio and television tower, Kaknästornet (► 129).

Summer in Stockholm – ideally in a little wooden house on a skerry island

FEELING

OUT IN THE SKERRIES

The Stockholmers love the water and the skerries (➤21). Many of the capital's inhabitants have a weekend house out on one of the islands, which they cross over to in their own boat, on the ferry, or aboard an excursion boat. Why don't you stay a few days? You can also rent holiday homes on the skerries.

FINGER FOOD

Part of the Stockholmers' new savoir vivre means that shopping no longer entails just wandering through a market hall. A canapé here, a titbit there, a food sample over there: Stockholm's everyday snacks have also been transformed into refined street food. The market hall on Östermalmstorg (➤65) is particularly popular.

That Stockholm Feeling

VIP-WATCHING ON THE STRANDVÄGEN

Strandvägen (▶ 63) is the most prestigious boulevard in Stockholm. Many stars and starlets stay in the magnificent buildings overlooking the sea. As do Sweden's well-to-do. The ship restaurants along the quay are the meeting place for everyone who wants to be seen sipping on a glass of Champagne. Why not join the cool crowd, don your sunglasses and order a glass of bubbly yourself? Those who only want to watch from the sidelines can sit on one of the numerous benches along the promenade, buy an ice-cream and view the strutting vanities.

NIGHTLIFE IN SOFO

It used to take a long time to find the in-districts in Stockholm. Going out was expensive – and anyone wanting to get into the upmarket bars had to get dressed up and join the long queue. Just meeting friends "for a beer" was not something people did. That changed a few years ago. In the nightlife district of SoFo (▶ 136) you will find nice pubs and cafés, but you can equally dance your way through the night. The Kvarnen beer hall (▶ 150), which also plays a role in the *Millennium* trilogy by Stieg Larsson is particularly popular.

SINGING ALONG IN SKANSEN

A real Swede always has a song on his lips. Every Tuesday evening in summer, thousands flock to the Skansen Open-Air Museum for the Allsång (▶ 19) to sing together. Even the TV crews are there. Even if you don't know the songs, it is worth passing by. It would be difficult to find a more authentic experience of Sweden.

OUT IN THE FRESH AIR

Swedes are fresh-air fanatics. Regardless what the weather is like, they want to be out jogging, skiing, cycling or doing other activities. However, there are more relaxing alternatives for the hours outside: a picnic with a cinnamon bun and coffee, the Swedish alternative to cheese and wine. (Drinking alcohol in public is forbidden.) People love the Rålambshovsparken on Kungsholmen. In Rålis, as the locals call it, you are even allowed to barbecue on the spaces designated for this purpose, whilst the youngsters can take advantage of the skate-boarding track.

Chilling in the afternoon in Café String, one of many top addresses in SoFo's nightlife district

The Magazine

WATER EVERYWHERE

Regardless of whether you are off to Lake Malär or the Baltic Sea, it does not take long to reach the water here. Stockholm is a city surrounded by nature – and its inhabitants are proud of their first urban national park.

There have been many songs sung about Stockholm's 54 bridges. And you need the many bridges because Stockholm is an island beauty; 14 inhabited islands belong to the city district. It is not surprising that with so much water, you often hear it referred to as the "Venice of the North". The sobriquet was even used for a long time in Stockholm, but has in the meantime become slightly hackneyed. Stockholm's self-confidence has grown and people have come to realise that Stockholm does not need to allude to the lagoon town in northern Italy at all. In terms of beauty, Stockholm can take on every city in the world – without any comparisons at all.

200 Years of Peace

The fact that Sweden has not waged any wars for over 200 years is evident from the capital. When you walk through Gamla Stan, the old town of Stockholm, you almost expect a horse and carriage to come rattling towards you round the next corner, or to see a market-woman carrying plucked chickens and an artisan dressed in traditional costume. Little has changed in the narrow streets over the centuries. Admittedly, souvenir shops have moved into the former workshops of blacksmiths and cobblers,

From the Skeppsholmsbron, you can look down on the Old Town and towards the Royal Palace

and tourists have replaced farmers and fishermen. The pace of life has also changed – everything has to move much faster. Today Stockholm, tomorrow Rome. That is the slogan of modern cruise ships. Yet in the evenings when the shops are shut and the tourists have disappeared into their hotels, then the clocks turn back and it looks as though you have been catapulted into the Middle Ages.

Faith in the Future and Renewal Mania

Stockholm also bears scars. However, the Swedish capital suffered these injuries at the hands of the town planners. One could almost believe that after World War II they were envious of other countries, where the bombs and grenades had left behind a field of destruction but also space for a new beginning for architectural ideas. Although Stockholm was not destroyed during the War, the powers at be wanted to give it a new start.

The plan was to build a new Stockholm within 30 years, a modern city that could face the challenges of the future. In order to achieve this, it was necessary to liberate things from the old. The demolition was ruthless and showed no respect for history. In Hötorget (▶ 57), for instance, an established 17th-century district had to make room for five office towers. Stockholm's suburbs developed during this period. In the government's "Million Homes Programme", the plan was to build one million new flats within ten years. Given that the entire Swedish population at the time totalled 7.8 million, it was a gigantic project. Set up on open fields, the outcome was unendearing: satellite towns with poor quality housing blocks. Today, it is precisely these parts of the town that have the largest social problems. One consolation in the urban disaster was that owing to

Sergels torg in Norrmalm provides a contrast to "old" Stockholm

the oil crisis, the renewal programme conceived as a thirty-year project ran out of money halfway through and thus lost momentum. In 1974, the Kulturhuset (Culture House) was erected at Sergels torg – then work finished. Building has naturally continued in the city, but there is now less megalomania and more visual judgement.

Green Capital

Modern Stockholm is an environmentally friendly city. In professional circles, it is currently the new district of Hammarby Sjöstad that is making headline news. Here, around 9,000 flats have been built to accommodate around 20,000 people. And not just run-of-the-mill accommodation either, but homes that meet the strictest international environmental standards – with around 50% less energy consumption compared with the average Swedish flat. In the district's car pool, the inhabitants share vehicles and the rubbish is transported off the premises in subterranean pipelines. Goal for 2050: Stockholm will have given up fossil fuels entirely.

City Toll

With the introduction of the City Toll in 2007, the authorities initially made themselves very unpopular with the electorate. In the meantime, however, the toll system for driving into the city centre has been completely accepted; traffic has been reduced by 20%. However, the fact that even in Stockholm the ecological miracle has yet to occur is clear as soon as you get caught up in the rush hour traffic. Despite the investments in new cycle paths and the city toll, traffic still sits bumper to bumper driving into the city.

National Park in the City

There is a national park in Stockholm as well, and it is not located miles outside the town but on the edge of the city centre. The ecological park is the first and, until now, only urban national park in the world and has been open since the mid-1990s. Surprising: three quarters of all the native animals of Central Sweden have also made their home here in the Swedish capital.

The Humlegården in Östermalm: Stockholm boasts an abundance of green space

Swedes like to be out and about, and this is clearly demonstrated in Stockholm. In the 26 large city parks, you will see the inhabitants of the capital walking, jogging and cycling, or equipped with a picnic blanket, biscuits and a thermos flask. It is obvious to everyone at a glance: Stockholm is a green city. The view from the air reveals that Stockholm is one third built-up area, one-third green area and one-third water. After all, the Baltic is right on the doorstep and the almost 30,000 skerries (► 22) provide the Stockholmers with a great big recreational area. They go out to the islands on their boats in the summer, and in the winter the frozen sea provides a hiking route, cross-country skiing trails and ice-skating rink. When the ocean is not sufficient, then there is always Lake Mälar, the country's third largest lake. Its water is so clean that it is possible to fish for salmon in the city centre. That isn't possible in Venice.

THE MOST BEAUTIFUL PARKS IN STOCKHOLM

- **Djurgården** (► 109)
- **Hagaparken** (► 54)
- **Humlegården**: The little park is a green oasis in the centre of the town. It originally provided the location for the royal vegetable garden, in which apparently hops were also cultivated. That is exactly what the Swedish word *humle* means. In the centre of the park is the Kungliga biblioteket, the Royal Library, which is home to a collection of more than 20 million books.
- **Tantolunden**: Located on the Södermalm Island, Tantolunden is one of the largest parks in the town. Near the pubs and restaurants of Mariatorget, it is popular with young people who congregate here before (or after) their pub tour. In summer, the attractions are the bathing spots and in winter Stockholm's best toboggan runs.
- **Observatorielunden** (► 69): This park is centrally located near Odenplans – and yet it soon makes you feel miles away from the hustle and bustle of the big city. From the 42m (138ft) high observatory hill, from which the park takes its name, you can enjoy a beautiful view over the eastern part of the town.

From **Stronghold** to **Capital**

The heart of the town beats on the islands of Stadsholmen, Helgeandsholmen and Riddarholmen, which still form the historic centre. Yet Stockholm has long since burst beyond these narrow boundaries to become Sweden's largest city, extending in the meantime over 14 islands.

There are many, in part contradictory, stories about how Stockholm came into being, but they all focus on the location's important economic and strategic control of the waterways. This connecting port between the Baltic and Lake Mälar was thus predestined to become a settlement. Around 1250, Birger Jarl had a castle built here, mentioned for the first time in a document in 1252, which is why this date is regarded as the year the town was founded and Jarl is seen as its founder (although excavations have indicated that there was a lake dwelling here from the 11th century).

The castle expanded to become the Tre Kronor fortress. The "three crowns" that represented the united kingdoms of Götaland, Svealand and Norrland are still included in Stockholm's coat of arms. The new town developed behind the protective walls of the fortress and was already recorded as the largest town in the kingdom in 1289. Since the king did not have a permanent seat of government there, the town was only important as a trade port. It was not until 1634 that Stockholm officially became the capital of the Swedish Empire.

Stockholm Bloodbath and Beginning of the Vasa Period

In 1397 Sweden joined the Kalmar Union, which was under the control of the Danish king, but there was nonetheless a strong urge for independence in Sweden. When the Danish king Christian II succeeded his father to the throne in 1513, Regent Sten Sture the Younger was governing Sweden. Three years later he was killed during the Battle of Bogesund, which made it possible to break down the resistance to the Danes and for Christian II to be crowned King of Sweden.

He had promised the rebels amnesty. However, after the three days of festivities, which were intended to support the reconciliation process, he had about 90 insurgents from the Swedish nobility executed on 8 November 1520. It went down in history as the "Stockholm Bloodbath". Christian II wanted to completely rid himself of any opposition, but in fact this episode

They left their mark on Stockholm: Birger Jarl (here as a statue on the square that bears his name) and Gustav III (in a portrait by Alexandre Roslin)

achieved quite the opposite. Following the Stockholm Bloodbath, Gustav Vasa headed the uprising that would liberate Sweden from the Kalmar Union. In addition to the bourgeoisie, the town was now distinguished by a royal court. The town's islands became too small, so Södermalm and Norrmalm were integrated in 1529.

Sweden's Time as a Ruling Power

The 17th century saw Sweden rise to become a major power. Stockholm grew at a tremendous pace and extended to include the islands of Östermalm and Kungsholmen. The capital's population increased six-fold during this period. Political ascendancy followed the economic success, and Stockholm developed into the centre of the Swedish kingdom and Baltic area.

The first crises followed in the early 18th century: in 1713 and 1714 the plague struck the city and the loss of land after the Great Northern War, 1721, led to stagnation in the town's economic development.

Under Gustav III, who became King of Sweden in 1771, Stockholm developed into a cultural centre. In 1786, Gustav III founded the Svenska Akademien (Swedish Academy) and initiated the golden age of Swedish language and literature. Expressing the architectural style of this period are the Royal Palace and the Royal Opera. The king loved the arts, wrote theatre plays himself and performed on stage as an actor. At the same time, he ruled as an absolute monarch and severely curbed the rights of the nobility. The latter would be his undoing; in 1792 he was murdered at a masked ball in a conspiracy initiated by the aristocracy. As a result, his ambitious building project, the palace in Haga Park, which he had conceived as Sweden's Versailles, was never completed.

Adversity and Affluence

From the beginning of the 19th century, poor peasant labourers poured into the town, which led to a rapid rise in the population and created a

Three generations of the Royal Family: Crown Princess Victoria and Prince Daniel with their children Oscar and Estelle as well as the royal couple Carl XVI Gustaf and Silvia (photo taken in July 2016)

sharp divide between Stockholm's rich and poor. The urban elite, comprising of merchants and intellectuals, prospered, attended glittering parties and generally enjoyed themselves, whilst the labourers and unemployed lived in squalor. In Gamla Stan and Södermalm, the conditions were particularly dramatic. With the streets full of rubbish and sewage, hygienic conditions were a catastrophe. Until 1861, Stockholm did not have sewers and was regarded as one of the dirtiest towns in Europe. The lack of sewers was the reason why cholera and other epidemics struck the town again and again.

On the Way to a Welfare State

More recent history has been kind to the town: Thanks to Sweden's neutrality in the two World Wars, Stockholm survived this time largely without any great damage, after which Sweden rose to become one of the richest industrial nations. While many parts of Europe had to focus on rebuilding, the Stockholmers could concentrate on developing their town and the welfare state.

Today Stockholm is a modern metropolis. Scandinavia's largest city is home to Sweden's parliament and government, and is the country's cultural centre. It has a constitutional monarchy; the king and his family have no political power. They represent their country in the same way as Queen Elizabeth II. And the Swedes love their royal family. Anyone who would like to see this for themselves should come to Stockholm when Crown Princess Victoria celebrates her birthday and thousands gratulate her and cheer.

SPLASHING & FLIRTING

Kungsträdgården is a popular meeting place. In the middle of the square, children splash around in the water basins in summer, and in winter they skate round the ice rink.

The long-haired woman in close-fitting business attire spoons her salad out of a plastic container. The man in a suit sitting next to her has different taste in food: in front of him on the ground is a bag from a large burger chain. The couple are having an animated conversation in the midday sun, and so engrossed in it that they don't even notice the children tumbling around in the water.

Kungsträdgården is Stockholm's beating heart. That can really be taken literally. People come here to dream, to relax, or to fall in love. Everyone seems to have time here. The summer lunch breaks last for ages. Blonde beauties show off their brown legs, but older gentlemen also wear shorts – everyone wants to get a bit of sun.

Kungsträdgården acts likes a magnet for both young and old. And that despite the fact that it is an austere idyll in the city centre. The first impression of the 200m (656ft) long and 50m (165ft) wide square is not that impressive: lots of concrete, a rather unattractive water basin with a few spluttering fountains and snack bars dotted along the sides. Stockholm has a lot of other squares that are more attractive.

This is where people get together – the Kungsträdgården in the centre of Stockholm

The Magazine

Fighting for Trees

However, perhaps the Stockholmers have such a soft spot for Kungsträdgården because they once campaigned for this square and the preservation of its trees. They are particularly fond of the large elms. The old gnarly trees were the heroes in the Elm Battle of 1971. At the time, the city planners intended to place the metro exit exactly where the trees grow. They were in the way and were to be cut down. However, they had not reckoned with the reaction of the Stockholmers. They stood up for their elms and climbed up into their branches. The tree fellers contracted by the municipal authorities had to leave with their chainsaws, their task undone. It became obvious that the municipal authorities had no desire to get involved in a long battle. Whilst in other places, they might have had the police march in, here they just gave in to the public's wish. The matter was resolved in two days. The metro exit was moved to another location.

Kungsträdgården's story goes far further back however. It was once the king's park, laid out during the reign of Eric of Pomerania, the first King of the Nordic Kalmar Union, in the 15th century. At that time, it was strictly forbidden for common people to enter the "royal park". The king strolled through the little wood, in the greenhouse his flowers blossomed, and the cabbages that His Majesty had grown for the royal saucepan flourished. Later rulers gradually extended Kungsträdgården into a wonderful park, which had a little castle, although there is nothing left of the little castle today.

At the beginning of the 19th century almost all of the trees were cut down. The idea was to let light and air flow through the park; the royal greenhouse was transformed into a dance hall. A few decades later, the walls surrounding the park were torn down and all the Stockholmers could visit it. At the same time, even more trees were cut down; the park became a "People's Square".

And that is what Kungsträdgården has remained until this day. In summer, it is transformed into a large open-air restaurant and in the evening into a party mile. Many of those who have spent their lunch break here come back to dine and party in the evening – and perhaps mingling among the guests of the park's restaurant or music pavilion are the flirting colleagues who sat on the steps of the Kungsträdgården that day so engrossed in their conversation.

FESTIVALS IN KUNGSTRÄDGÅRDEN

- On 30 April the city celebrates both the **Turkish Cultural Festival** and **Children's Day.**
- In the first week of June the festival **Smacka på Stockholm** (A Taste of Stockholm) is all about food (www.smakapastockholm.se).
- At the **Stockholm Street Festival** street artists and musicians perform on four days at the beginning of July (http://stockholmstreetfestival.com).
- **Free concerts** take place many times a year.

And Everyone Sings Along

Since 1935, Skansen Open-Air Museum has regularly had a second role as a huge open-air stage. Over 10,000 hobby singers meet here once a week for a sing-along. Swedish television has covered the event for almost 40 years.

Every Tuesday Grete Heiberg sets off in the direction of Skansen (➤ 109), the large open-air museum and zoo on the edge of Stockholm. Grete Heiberg is neither interested in the old buildings, nor is she interested in elk, bears, or wolves. The 67-year-old pensioner goes to Skansen once a week to attend the Allsång, a typical Swedish event. Translated into English, *allsång* literally means "singing together" – and sing-alongs are as much a part of the Swedish summer as the long days and the mosquitoes. Regardless of whether they are residents of a small village or a big city – Swedes get together to sing traditional Swedish songs.

Fun for Old and Young Alike
The largest Allsång Arena is in Stockholm – at the Skansen Open-Air Museum, and up to 15,000 people flock there on Tuesday evenings

Even Swedish stars sing along: Eurovision Song Contest Winner Måns Zelmerlöw at the Allsång på Skansen 2015

The Magazine

during the summer. To ensure that everyone hits the right note, stars from the Swedish music scene stand on the stage at the front and lead the melody. Unlike England where, apart from The Last Night of the Proms, singing traditional English melodies is not seen as being very cool by the younger generation, folk songs and Swedish hits are also popular with people under 30. Singing is something that is enjoyed by all generations. Most of the songs trilled at the Allsång are party hits. However, to ensure that everyone can really sing along, people at the Skansen sell pamphlets with the song texts. The sales are not that good though, because hardly anyone needs them as they do indeed know the words, just like Agnetha, Grete Heiberg's 40-year-old daughter. The 13-year-old granddaughter never misses the sing-along on Tuesday evenings either.

They share their hobby with innumerable other Swedes. Stockholm is the global capital for choir singing. Nowhere else in the world has as many choirs. All over Sweden, more than 600,000 people sing in an official choir. Given the fact that Sweden's total population is just over nine million, that is a considerable percentage. Most of them sing in church choirs, at school or in the university. But also almost every profession, from bus driver to teacher or fireman, has their own choir. Even tax office employees meet to sing together.

Singing Overlooking the City

The open-air stage in Skansen is located in one of the most beautiful places in Stockholm. From a hill outside the centre, visitors can enjoy a spectacular view of the sea, of the ferries on the way to Finland and of the Old Town. The "song arena" in Skansen thus offers a nice place to linger. And it is necessary too: Anyone who wants to have one of the places at the front has to get there early. You can use the time to have a picnic. Even on this mild summer evening, Grete Heiberg has coffee and *kanelkakor* (cinnamon biscuits) packed in her picnic basket. Singing is hard work, and a rumbling stomach would only disturb the concert. After two hours, several cups of coffee and lots of *kanelkakor*, the crowd gets going. The sing-along is just about to start. Presenter Sanna Nielsen comes up onto the state, the orchestra begins to play *Stockholm i mitt hjärta (Stockholm in my heart)* – and Grete Heiberg joins in with the same fervour as every Tuesday.

ALLSÅNG ON THE RADIO AND TV

Those who cannot be present can sing in front of the television. Allsång på Skansen is broadcast live on Swedish television and is the absolute quota hit. About a third of the Swedish population are sitting in front of the box when *Stockholm i mitt hjärta* goes on air. And it has been the same since 1979. Before that, the radio brought the sing-along to the lounge, accompanied by musicians who set the tone. Even today, the live broadcast still has an additional educational purpose, since all the song texts, like Karaoke, are included as subtitles.

Little
Getaways

Few Stockholmers would contemplate spending a summer weekend in the city. They prefer to take a boat to the skerries. The author of this travel guide accompanied them and wrote down his experiences.

I am in the crowd of people who set off on a Saturday morning with a picnic bag in hand and a daypack on their back towards the pier in front of the Dramaten, Stockholm's venerable theatre. It is from there that the excursion boats set off for the skerries. Those working during the Swedish summer and thus staying in town come here, at least at the weekends. Spending the summer in the city is not something the Stockholmers want to do. A trip with the boat out to the "Skerry Garden", Stockholm Archipelago offers a little escape.

Anyone who is particularly impatient unpacks his thermos flask and sandwiches while he leaves the harbour. Coffee aroma wafts over the ship and the second breakfast on board demands the full attention of many of the passengers. Stockholm's beauties pass by unnoticed by many of the day-trippers. No wonder: They have travelled out to the skerries hundreds of times. Perhaps they are among the happy souls who own a little weekend house on one of the islands.

I always find the trip through the waterways in the city centre absolutely fascinating. So I let my stomach rumble and postpone my breakfast till later. I enjoy the trip out of the harbour, the view on the right of the palace and the modern art museum. Museum Moderna Museet. Or on the left of the Djurgården island, the home of the Nordic Museum, the ABBA Museum, the Skansen Open-Air Museum, the *Vasa* battleship and the amusement park Gröna Lund.

30,000 Islands, 50,000 Holiday Homes, 150,000 Boats

All of Stockholm seems to be up on this summer morning and fleeing the mainland – almost as if the news had announced that a hurricane was coming or a volcano had erupted. An armada of leisure boats set course for the Stockholm skerries. But there is no danger. Nobody is really fleeing. Those out on the water are full of anticipation and looking

The Magazine

forward to a weekend by the sea. To sausages sizzling on the barbecue, to time with the family, with friends or just to time to themselves.

There are 150,000 privately owned boats in Stockholm. They all seem to be on the water today. But there is enough room for them all on the islands. After all, there are almost 30,000 of them in the sea off Stockholm, big and small, forested and unforested, inhabited and uninhabited. And new additions come along all the time. They develop very slowly of course. During the last Ice Age, Scandinavia was covered in huge icebergs. Their weight pushed the land masses downwards. After the icebergs melted the land rose again slowly. This process is still continuing in the Stockholm archipelago; there has been a 30cm (1ft) rise – although it should be added that this has been over a period of 100 years. Over the course of the next millennia further islands will arise from the water.

The number of houses on the skerries is formidable. 50,000 holiday homes are registered there. In purely mathematical terms that is not even two houses per island. Of course, the houses are distributed differently. And Robinson Crusoe would not feel happy on every island.

Inspiration for Artists

As soon as the ship leaves the inner harbour, nature takes over the command in terms of colour palette. It specifies the background colours: blue and green for water and woods. Man is only able to add individual dashes of colour. Yellow and red for the houses on the islands, white for the boats and sails on the sea.

The colours alone have always brought artists out to the skerry islands. There, they found inspiration, could sit on the pier lost in thought, breathe in the fresh air, let the sun shine on their forehead and listen to the screeching of the seagulls. Writers like August Strindberg for example. In the foreword of his novel *The People of Hemsö*, he writes that the Stockholm archipelago had always held a great fascination for him.

BOAT EXCURSIONS

■ The ships of **Waxholmsbolaget** (www.waxholmsbolaget.se) are the equivalent of city buses for the skerry inhabitants. They run – as far as winter ice allows – the year round and set course for almost every inhabited island off the coast of Stockholm. The departure is Strömkajen near Kungsträdgården in front of the Grand Hôtel.

■ The **Strömma** shipping company (www.stromma.se) runs a regular service with the Cinderellabåtar to the most important skerry islands. In addition, it organises excursion trips for tourists to the skerries in the Baltic and the Mälaren, to Drottningholm and Gripsholm castles, to the Viking island of Birka and through the Djurgården Canal. The departure points for trips to the Baltic are located on Nybrokajen along the Strandvägen. For trips on Lake Mälar, the steamers leave from the Stadshusbron, just a few metres away from the Stockholm City Hall. The canal tour begins at Strömkajen.

After a good hour, our boat docks for the first time. The picnic things are hastily packed away in the basket and the first Stockholmers go ashore. After another half an hour I have arrived at my destination. Ten other people leave the boat with me. From the pier, I ramble along a little path in the woods. When I turn around a short while later I realise that everyone else has disappeared. I wonder whether the little red house next to the dock belongs to them. I, at any rate, am now on my own. I have the island to myself. I reach the other side after ten minutes. There, I decide to do the same as the great artists. Like them, I looked for inspiration. The sun and the sea will support me in this – as will the contents of my picnic basket.

In the "Skerry Garden", Stockholm archipelago – the rural idyll on the doorstep of the Swedish metropolis

August Strindberg
A Man of Extremes

When August Strindberg died in Stockholm on 14 May 1912, it marked the end of an eventful life full of contradictions. Strindberg was a pacifist, socialist and supporter of woman's emancipation – a conservative, misogynist and occultist. But above all, he was a man constantly searching for the truth.

August Strindberg was born into a humble household in 1849, his father was a trader and his mother a maid. The relationship with his parents, especially his father, can be safely described as tense. After completing secondary school and briefly studying medicine and literature at university, Strindberg tried his hand at acting. He was brought back to earth with a bump during the audition at the Royal Dramatic Theatre, which he failed so miserably that he even contemplated suicide. Despite his failure, Strindberg's excursion into the world of acting did not remain without its benefits, because it led to his decision to become a playwright. In 1870 his one-act play *In Rome* was performed on stage for the first time and received positive reviews. A year later, his play *The Outlaw* actually earned him a grant to continue his studies. He also found a job in the Royal

Library in Stockholm during this period, which meant that he at last had a sound financial basis.

Three Marriages

In 1875 he made the acquaintance of an actress called Siri von Essen and married her two years later. Following their divorce in 1891, Strindberg married another two times: his next wife was the journalist Frida Uhl and, in 1901, he wed Harriet Bosse, who was also an actress.

His novel, *The Red Room*, a satire of Swedish society was published in 1879. Today the book is regarded as a masterpiece of realism. During Strindberg's lifetime, opinion was mixed and those who had come under attack struck back with a vengeance. This induced the sensitive writer to "flee" the country to Switzerland. Yet Sweden's general public continued to pursue the author, even accusing him of blasphemy for expressions used in his collection of short stories *Getting Married*.

STRINDBERG MUSEUM (STRINDBERGSMUSEET)

From 1908 to 1912 August Strindberg lived in the so-called Blue Tower at no 85 Drottninggatan (✚ 179 D2; tel: 08 4 11 53 54; www.strindbergs museet.se, Tue–Sun noon–4pm, metro Rådmansgatan, entry fee kr75). Today, it houses a museum dedicated to the playwright, which i.a. showcases his recreated home interior, his original furniture and last but not least his library of 3,000 books.

August Strindberg at his desk (undated photograph)

Model Nietzsche

At the end of the 1880s, there was a decisive change in Strindberg's character, and one that was very much reflected in his work. Under the influence of Nietzsche, his socialist views were transformed into an adoration of "intellectual aristocrats" and what he called *Übermenschen* or "superior beings". It was also at this point that the misogyny, for which Strindberg is still known today, came to the fore.

Having led a nomadic life for many years, Strindberg finally returned to Stockholm in 1899. In the early years of the 20th century, Strindberg's stage works were of a surreal-symbolic character, which reflected Strindberg's own inner conflict after the failure of his marriage with Harriet Bosse.

He spent the last years of his life in his "Blue Tower" in Drottninggatan in Stockholm. This was, however, not an ivory tower in which he hid from the world. On the contrary, it was here that, in his later years, he led an embittered campaign against the fossilised Swedish society of which he was a particularly fierce critic. Strindberg was particularly offended that – despite being one of the greatest playwrights of the time – he never received the Nobel Prize for Literature. If nothing else at least, on his 63rd birthday, just a few months before his death, his followers handed him a kind of "Anti-Nobel Prize" with which they honoured his ground-breaking oeuvre.

GALLERY IN THE METRO

Stockholm's Tunnelbana is not only the fastest mode of transport in the Swedish capital, it is also a work of art. Stockholmers proudly boast that their metro is the longest gallery in the world. Almost all of the 100 stations have in the meantime been embellished with fanciful sculptures, light installations, paintings, mosaics, engravings and reliefs.

The idea to liberate tubes from their sad and boring existence is neither new nor unique. A classic example is the Moscow Metro opened in 1935, which provides pleasure to its passengers with its Baroque splendour and chandeliers. In Vienna, too, taking the underground is well worthwhile. Art Nouveau motifs decorating the entrances lead the way down to the trains. In Lisbon, a trip takes you through the contemporary art of Hundertwasser and Calatrava. However, Stockholm's Tunnelbana has no reason to be reticent. Back in the 1950s, builders had already started to remove cold neon lights, dreary tiled walls and billboards. "Art for the Masses" was the latest thing at the time, and what was more natural than to exhibit art in public transport facilities used day in and day out by thousands of people. Collaboration between architects, engineers and artists had been working well for quite some time already, since there was a regulation that 1% of the funds for the public building project was to be used for artistic design. For the Tunnelbana project, this sum was actually doubled.

The Solna centrum station – a "Nightmare in Green and Blood Red"

The Bathroom Stations

The T-Centralen Station is the central junction of Stockholm's metro
network. This is where all three lines, the Red, the Green and the
Blue come together. T-Centralen is not only vital in terms of the transport system, it also provided the initial impulse for the art project,
because it was here with the station's tiled walls that metro art got
going in the 1950s.

It would not remain the only station with decorative tiles, Hötorget is
another example. The Stockholmers soon nicknamed these stops the
"Bathroom Stations". The name has stuck although in the meantime
T-Centralen has a lot more than tiles on offer. Against a white background,
cobalt blue glows on the tunnel walls in the cavernous, grotto-like hall.
The 1975 motif chosen by artist Per Olof Ultvedt depicts silhouettes of
construction workers sawing and hammering, which is in homage to the
people that built the Tunnelbana. Another of his motifs includes the floral
creepers, also in blue and white; they are intended to help passengers
feel more relaxed.

The Blue Line

Anyone who does not have much time, or is in Stockholm for the first time,
should at least travel on the Blue Line from Kungsträdgården to Akalla and
Hjulsta. Almost every station displays an interesting artwork, surprising,
fascinating, dramatic or all three. A convincing victory over the monotony
of public transport.

A particular highlight is the cave-like Kungsträdgården station designed
by Ulrik Samuelson. Here, you find yourself plunged into a mystical
grotto landscape with Baroque sculptures, real ivy and rippling rivulets.
Samuelson's goal was to create a metro garden that would remind people
of the Royal Baroque park, the Kungsträdgården, that used to be above it.
The artist gave each detail a symbolic meaning: the gas lamps once used
to light the Torsgatan, the pattern on the floor represents the garden.

Cave Paintings

Since the metro art was, on the whole, being received with great enthusiasm, the authorities took the project a step further and designed holistic
concepts for the new stations on which artists, architects and technicians
worked together from the very beginning. From then on, art was not a
subsequent embellishment of a building project but an integral component
of it. Examples of this include the stations Rådhuset, Näckrosen and Solna
centrum. At Solna centrum the artists Karl-Olov Björk and Anders Åberg
created a red, cave-like ceiling and wall paintings depicting a coniferous
forest which they have called *Sweden in the Seventies*. Many people still
perceive the station as a nightmare in green and blood red. This actually
corresponds to a large extent with the intention of the artists. Their concept
was to illustrate in gloomy pictures the destruction of nature, the pollution
of waterways and the death of the forests.

The Magazine

On a Discovery Tour

Just get into a train in the Stockholmer Tunnelbana and let it take you somewhere. You will constantly come across astonishing artworks and details. At the Rådmansgatan station, Strindberg's piercing eyes indicate the way to his museum. Tekniska högskolan, in contrast, displays a strictly geometric design. At the Stadion station, a rainbow adorning the rough tunnel walls pervades the space with cheerfulness and optimism. Further works by Enno Hallek and Åke Pallarp, who created a tribute to the 1912 Summer Olympics in 1973, are also among the metro's most colourful.

Although the art in the Stockholm metro is not the only example of its kind, the number of artworks, the long tradition and the fusion of art and architecture makes it absolutely unique.

Wall paintings in the Kungsträdgården and T-Centralen stations

28

Meatballs
&
Award-Winning Cuisine

Stockholm is turning into a gourmet paradise, but still holds fast to its traditions.

Stars galore glitter over Stockholm. Nine restaurants sport Michelin stars, two of them can boast a pair. In addition, the Frantzén restaurant (▶95) is currently ranked 23 in the list of the world's best restaurants. And: Sweden's national team of chefs regularly takes part in the Culinary Olympics – yes, it does exist – and is often among the winners. Sweden, with Stockholm as its flag bearer, is now in a completely new culinary class. From a country, known for its greasy meatballs and not very appetising sausages to a country whose culinary specialities are taking the global scene by storm. No small contributor to this no doubt is the Swedish countryside that provides top chefs with the finest and freshest produce.

While not rating as high-end gastronomy, Sweden's traditional fare has its merits too. Anyone who has come to Sweden aboard

Swedish classic: *köttbullar* with mashed potato and *gravad lax*

a boat has probably become acquainted with the *smörgåsbord* (Swedish for "bread table"), Sweden's typical self-service buffet with its large selection of delicious cold and hot dishes. It dates back to the traditional farmers' parties where the entire village got together and each guest brought along a meal. In those days, everything was put on a big table and everyone dug in to the gluttonous feast.

The Magazine

Mr Jansson's Temptation

The real *smörgåsbord* specialist adheres to a particular system when he feasts. There is no arbitrary piling on of dishes willy-nilly. You start with the fish dishes, then proceed to the cold starters before serving yourself a hot main course, which is then rounded off with a dessert and a small piece of cheese. Meatballs, *köttbullar*, also belong to a *smörgåsbord*, which due to the high-fat examples sold on the street stands have sacrificed a bit of their good reputation. They are eaten with mashed potato, *potatismos*.

Another classic in the traditional fare – *Janssons frestelse*, Jansson's temptation – is a potato gratin with onions, anchovies and a rich creamy sauce. When smoked herring is used instead of anchovies, then the Swedes call it *Karlssons frestelse*, and when it does not include any fish at all, it is called *Svenssons frestelse*. The problem with all three variations is the sauce, which is so rich that its taste completely dominates the meal. Anyone watching their pennies when ordering food tends to pick *pytt i panna*. That is generally the least expensive dish on the menu. A translation of the name, which reveals how it is prepared, explains the price: "Into the pan with the leftovers". It generally consists of potatoes, sausages, leftover roasts, mixed together with peas and onions. A fried egg is served on top, perhaps to conceal the hotchpotch beneath.

Naturally, Sweden is also renowned for its excellent fish dishes. *Gravad lax* is a fresh, marinated salmon, seasoned with salt, sugar, pepper and predominantly dill. It is served with boiled potatoes. The name dates back to the days when people did not have fridges. During that time *gravad lax* was anything but fresh, rather – as the Swedish word indicates – "buried". Cleaning the fish, seasoning it and then burying it was the best way to preserve it. *Strömming*, Baltic herring is the proletarian brother of the fine salmon. It is served either fried or pickled.

Smelly Fish with Flight Ban

It should not be confused with *surströmming*. The "sour herring" originally comes from the north of Sweden, but is eaten everywhere in Sweden. It is one of the most foul-smelling fish in the world. Herring caught in the early summer are marinated in a brine solution in a wooden barrel. After about a month, the fish is put into tins, where the fermentation process continues. When a *surströmming tin* bulges, there is no reason to worry. That is the way it should be and just indicates that the fish is ready to eat. You are not allowed to take *surströmming* on a plane. Anyone who has ever tasted it knows why. And another tip: To avoid the foul-smelling liquid from squirting, it is better to open the tin under water.

Why do the Swedes love this smelly fish so much that they dedicate a whole festival to it, the *surströmmingspremiären* on the third Thursday in August? Perhaps it is due to the fact that the fermented fish is washed down with a big glass of Schnapps.

Bistro Oaxen Slip in Djurgården offers first-class cuisine in industrial warehouse ambience

The Magazine

Crispbread, only Real with a Hole

What else does Swedish cooking have to offer? The Swedes generally bake their bread with syrup, so that it tastes unusually sweet while the butter is salted, and there is a much larger selection of yoghurts and milk drinks than in Britain. Pea soup is a traditional dish on Thursdays. And then there is the crispbread, probably Sweden's biggest export hit in the last centuries.

This type of bread, which keeps fresh for a long time, was "invented" on Swedish farms. In the winter, the rivers and streams froze, so that it was not possible to grind flour. That is why in the autumn people started baking crispbread to last them through the winter. When it was ready it was hung on a pole along the kitchen wall. That kept it away from the mice and always within reach. Whenever the Swedes were hungry, all they had to do was to break off or *knäcka* a piece, which is how it earned its Swedish name *knäckebröd*.

These days, the hole in the middle of the crispbread no longer makes sense. Crispbread baked in this way, for a long time purely for nostalgic reasons, was just impractical. It did not fit in the bread bin and wasted a lot of space during transport. In 2005, crispbread in its original shape disappeared completely from the shop shelves in Sweden, which immediately led to protests from traditionalists. Internet forums were set up in which crispbread fans fulminated about the discontinuation of the round crispbread. Signatures were even gathered. However, it did not change anything: the round crispbread became the latest victim of modern times and, at least in the supermarket, is no longer available.

Connoisseurs of fine caviar are in the right place in Sweden (left). Crispbread (right) was traditionally kept on a pole

Finding Your Feet

First Two Hours

Only those planning to do a tour round Sweden or Scandinavia as a whole should consider driving the car. The journey is very arduous, and drivers in Stockholm soon discover that parking space is both rare and extremely costly.

Arrival by Plane

- Stockholm's main airport **Arlanda** (www.swedavia.se/arlanda) is located a good 35km (22mi) north of the centre of the main town.
- **Direct flights** are available from London to Stockholm with **British Airways** (www.britishairways.com) and **SAS** (www.flysas.com) as well as other airlines and budget companies such as **Monarch** (www.monarch.co.uk) and **Ryanair** (www.ryanair.com). The flight takes just over two hours.
- Flights are provided **from the USA and Canada** to Stockholm-Arlanda International Airport by a number of airlines including Condor, KLM, Delta and United Airlines. Many other airlines offer indirect flights. There are no direct flights from **Australia**.
- The no-frills airline Ryanair flies from London Stansted to **Stockholm-Skavsta**, which is located 100km (62mi) south of Stockholm by Nyköping.

Airport Transfer by Taxi

The taxi ride from Arlanda airport to the city centre takes about half an hour. The trip costs about kr500–kr600. Taxi Stockholm (➤ 36) offers a fixed price of kr520.

Airport Transfer by Train

- The train connection with **Arlanda Express** (www.arlandaexpress.com) to the main station takes about 20 minutes. It runs from Arlanda between 5:05am and 0:35am, from the main station between 4:35am and 0:35am.
- The train departs at least three times an hour. A **single ticket** costs kr280, a **return** kr540; children and young adults under 26 kr150/kr300. From Tuesday till Sunday, two people travelling together pay only kr300 for a joint ticket; discounts are often available for online bookings as well.

Flight Transfer by Bus

- The transfer with the shuttle service offered by **Flygbussarna Airport Coaches** (www.flygbussarna.se) lasts about 40 minutes. The single trips costs kr119, and a return trip kr215; travellers under 17 pay kr99/kr179. Online tickets are slightly cheaper.
- The bus runs about every ten minutes (later in the evening after the arrival of each flight) from Arlanda to the **Cityterminal** by the main station. The bus driver can arrange a Flygbussarna taxi for the journey from the main station to the hotel.
- Buses also travel between Arlanda and the suburbs of **Bromma** and **Täby Centrum** as well as the **trade fair**.
- From the more distant **Skavsta Airport** to Stockholm Cityterminal, the bus trip lasts about one and a half hours. On a positive note, however, the return ticket at kr285 costs only slightly more than from Arlanda.

Insider Tip

Arrival by Train

There are **regular train connections** to Stockholm from London by Eurostar.
If you have time to spare, it makes a wonderful alternative because there
are plenty of places along the way, where you could consider making a stop,
such as Hamburg or Copenhagen. A number of these options, including
a Dutch Flyer train & ferry combination, are listed on the following website:
https://www.seat61.com/Sweden.htm.

Tourist Information

Kulturhuset, Sergels torg 3–5; tel: 08 50 82 85 08, mid-Sep–April.
Mon–Fri 9am–6pm, Sat 9am–4pm, Sun 10am–4pm, May–mid-Sep
Mon–Fri 9am–7pm, Sat 9am–4pm (July, Aug until 6pm), Sun 10am–4pm;
www.visitstockholm.com.

Getting Around

**The public local transport system in Stockholm is excellent, but the fare
system is very complicated – buying tickets can turn out to be a real obstacle
course for non-Swedes.**

Tickets in Public Local Transport

■ Since almost every Stockholmer buys his ticket via app or SMS with his
  mobile phone (only possible with a Swedish SIM card) or the SL-Card,
  a chipcard that deducts the price of the fare, the service has become
  increasingly bad for all other customers. Those who don't want to end
  up paying more need to prepare a bit in advance.
■ Those only intending to use public transport for a few journeys are better
  off buying single tickets. In the city area, these cost kr36 when bought
  in advance from *pressbyråen* (news kiosks) or from the ticket vending
  machines, or kr50 directly at the ticket barrier. Within the duration of the
  ticket's validity of 75 minutes, you can change trains as often as you like
  and even return along the same route.
■ No tickets are sold on the **buses** – anyone who gets on without one will
  be refused transportation.
■ Alternatives are the **24-hour ticket** for kr115 (people under 20 and over
  65 pay kr70), the **72-hour ticket** for kr230 (reduced kr140) and the
  weekly ticket for kr300 (reduced kr180).
■ It is only possible to buy some tickets, including the weekly ticket, if you
  have a **SL-Card**, which functions like a value/prepaid card.
■ These tickets can be bought from vending machines at the tube
  stations, from *pressbyråns* (news kiosks), in 7-Eleven shops and the
  SL-Info Centres (e.g. T-Centres, Slussen). Most of the tickets can be
  bought via the Internet, but only if you already have an SL card.
■ The penalty for fare dodging is kr600!

Metro (Tunnelbana)

■ Stockholm's tube stations, the **Tunnelbana**, are indicated with a blue T.
  The metro network comprises of three main lines (Green, Red and Blue),
  which cross at the central station, T-Centralen, and branch out beyond
  the city into auxiliary lines.

Finding Your Feet

- During the day, the trains run very frequently. Trains run Mon–Fri from 5am, Sat, Sun from 6am; on nights preceding work days, the last trains are around midnight or 1am, otherwise 3am or 3:30am.
- The Stockholm metro is sometimes referred to as the **longest art gallery in the world**; many stations have been upgraded with sculptures, mosaics, painting and installations (➤ 26).
- The Tunnelbana is supplemented by three **Pendeltåg** (shuttle train) lines as well as five **commuter trains**.

Buses

- Stockholm's **bus network** is excellent. Buses in the inner city have one- or two-digit numbers.
- **Night buses** travel from 1am from the stations Centralen (Vasagatan and Sergels torg), Slussen and Odenplan.
- When **exploring the city**, lines 44, 47 (to Djurgården) and 69 (to Kaknästornet) are important, because it is not possible to reach either of the two destinations on the metro.

Trams

- There are two lines in Stockholm. **Line 7** runs between Kungsträdgården and Waldemarsudde from 5:15am till 2am. **Nostalgia Tram 7N** (Djurgårdslinje) is a heritage tram with vintage wagons – the oldest dating back to the 1910s – that operates between Norrmalmstorg and Waldemarsudde (mid-June–end Aug daily, as well as Sep–mid-Dec and end March–mid-June on weekends and public holidays, each between 11am and 5pm/6pm/7pm, normal ticket price).
- The **suburban line 21** (Lindigöbahn) connects Ropsten and Gåshaga brygga.

Ferries

Naturally, ferries play an important role in a city spread over 14 islands. The **Djurgårdsfärjan** connects Slussen with Skeppsholmen and Djurgården, SL tickets are valid.

City Tours/City Walks

- Stockholm Sightseeing offers guided walks, bus and boat tours, all of which are available in English. These include city tours in open buses, which you can hop on and hop off as often as you like during the day, or combined panorama bus tours and walks with a visit to the palace (www.stromma.se).

Insider Tip
- Volunteers from Free Tours Stockholm provide, as the name reveals, free walking tours. An English-speaking guide takes visitors through Norrmalm, Gamla Stan and Södermalm (www.freetour stockholm.com).

Taxi

Insider Tip
- In Stockholm taxi companies are free to organise their own fare scheme. They are therefore **significant price differences** between the various companies. For this reason, you should always ask the price before getting into the taxi. (Most taxis have a sticker on their rear window with details of their prices.)
- Among the larger companies is **Taxi 020** (tel: 08 3 66 99), **Taxi Stockholm** (tel: 08 15 00 00; www.taxistockholm.se), **Topcap** (tel: 08 33 33 33), **Taxi Stockholm** (tel: 08 30 00 00).

Car

- Even if you have driven the car to Sweden, once you are in Stockholm you should **change to public city transport**. The distances in the town are generally short; the bus and metro networks are well-developed, parking spaces on the other hand are extremely expensive and few and far between.
- **Long-term parking** is available at the ferry terminals of Silja Line (Ropsten) and Viking Line (Södermalm), at Arlanda and Bromma airports and near the commuter train stations and metro stations (www.stockholmparkering.se).
- **Parking fees** can be paid with a credit card or with a mobile phone (Swedish SIM card necessary). Although there are coin pay stations in some of the carparks, they are gradually being removed.
- In 2007, Stockholm introduced a **City Toll**, which has been charged since early 2015 and is also collected from the owners of foreign vehicles (there is no toll due for motorcycles). The bill is done fully automatically. Photographs are taken of the registration number of each car passing the control station, and you then receive the bill by post. The **toll amount** depends on the time of day and the amount of traffic. The highest rate per day is kr105 – even when you drive in and out of Stockholm numerous times. The toll is charged from Mondays to Fridays from 6am–6:29pm. No charge is made on Saturdays, Sunday, public holidays and on working days that directly precede a public holiday, as well as the whole month of May. For further information, see http://transportstyrelsen.se.
- Anyone wishing to **hire a car**, can choose between the usual international rental companies and many local firms. The search words *hyra bil* or *hyrbil* will help to produce the results you want when you are researching on the Internet. It is often cheaper to book the car before you set off. For visitors only planning to tour the town, it is not worth hiring a car.

Cycling

- Stockholm is more or less flat and can boast a **very well-developed network of cycle paths**. The perfect conditions for exploring the city on two wheels.
- **Stockholm City Bikes**: Hiring bicycles from Stockholm City Bikes is not complicated. First of all, you need a rental card, which you can obtain from the Stockholm Tourist Centre, near Pressbyrån, 7-Eleven, the urban transport companies SL and at many hotels. It is either valid for three days (kr165) or for the entire season (kr300, kr250 when ordering online). It allows you to hire a bike from one of the around 70 bike stations in the city area from April till October (daily 6am–10pm, Return by 1am; www.citybikes.se).
- A selection of **further rental companies**:

Bike Sweden
✉ Narvavägen 13–17
☎ 08 52 52 70 00;
www.bikesweden.se

Djurgårdsbrons sjöcafé
✉ Galärvarvsvägen 2
☎ 08 66 05 75;
www.sjocafeet.se/en

Gamla Stans Cyke
✉ Stora Nygatan 20
☎ 08 4 11 16 70;
www.gamlastanscykel.se

Rent a Bike
✉ Strandvägen/Kajplats 18
☎ 08 6 60 79 59;
www.rentabike.se

Accommodation

Tourism is booming in Stockholm – and that practically all year round. This inevitably means that capacities are often exhausted fairly quickly. Especially during major events, it can be a problem to find a room that is more or less affordable.

- The price level is relatively high; you can save with family or weekend flat rates.
- In **summer** (mid-June to mid-August), when there are not as many business trips, the hotels also have special offers during the week.
- Swedish **youth hostels** (*vandrarhem*) have long since lost their reputation for having dreary rooms and bunkbeds. Accommodation here is relatively inexpensive, and the hostels generally have family rooms.
- **Destination Stockholm** offers the Stockholm Package, which includes accommodation, breakfast, sightseeing tours, free admission to museums as well as trips on "Hop On, Hop Off" bus and boat routes (www.destination-stockholm.com).

Accommodation Prices

For a double room with breakfast:

£ under kr1,000   ££ kr1,000–kr2,000   £££ over kr2,000

---

af Chapman £

The proud three-master, built in England in 1888 and converted into a youth hostel in 1949, lies at anchor off Skeppsholmen. Passengers sleep in cabins with two to fifteen beds and enjoy the maritime atmosphere and a fantastic view of Gamla Stan from the sun deck. Order well in advance!!

✚ 181 F3 ✉ Flaggsmansvägen 8
☎ 08 4 63 22 66;
www.stfchapman.com
🚇 Kungsträdgården 🚌 65

August Strindberg Hotell ££

Small (27 rooms) and simple, but quiet, central and familial, with stylish breakfast room. In the small inner courtyard, there is a bust commemorating Sweden's national poet. The beautiful old building dates back to the end of the 19th century and was once a tea factory. Anyone yearning for some greenery will find it in the nearby park.

✚ 178 C2 ✉ Tegnergatan 38
☎ 08 32 50 06; www.hotellstrindberg.se
🚇 Rådmansgatan 🚌 2

Best Western NoFo Hotel ££

Anyone wishing to party in the trendy SoFo district is in the perfect location here. Old but well-renovated building from 1780 that, over the years, has served as a brewery, poor house and hospital. Four-star level with a total of 46 rooms and an opulent breakfast buffet.

✚ 181 F1 ✉ Tjärhovsgatan 11
☎ 08 50 31 12 00; www.nofohotel.se
🚇 Medborgarplatsen

Birger Jarl Hotel £££

Some of Sweden's best designers and interior decorators have demonstrated their skills here. They often took their inspiration from the nature of the north. Fresh greens, bright autumn colours and natural materials round off the light and airy interior. The only anomaly: the *glömda rummet*, the room the craftsmen completely forgot about during the renovation work for the hotel because it was at the end of the corridor. Since no-one wanted to start all over again, the room was just cleaned up, and it maintained its 1970s design – much to the joy of the retro fans.

⊞ 179 D2 ✉ Tulegatan 8
☎ 08 6 74 18 00; www.birgerjarl.se
🚇 Rådmansgatan 🚌 2

Browallshof Hotell & Matsal ££

In 2014 this little hotel, which only has 17 rooms, was completely renovated without any of its charm being lost in the process. King Gustav III once stayed in the 1731 guesthouse. All of the rooms are furnished with 18th-century Gustavian style antiques; the kitchen serves quality traditional fare, and the sun terrace is made for relaxation.

⊞ 179 D3 ✉ Surbrunnsgatan 20
☎ 08 16 51 36; http://browallshof.se
🚇 Tekniska Högskolan

Clarion Hotel Sign £££

Star architect Gerd Wingårdh conceived something unusual for the design hotel at the station, a facade of glass and black granite, and angles that are seldom ninety degrees. The 558 rooms and suites exude an impressive, timeless elegance, which is not very surprising considering that they were conceived by design stars such as Bruno Mathsson, Alvar Aalto and Arne Jacobsen. The wellness oasis on the eighth floor from which you can view the entire town has a strong appeal.

⊞ 178 C1 ✉ Östra Järnvägsgatan 35
☎ 08 6 76 98 00; www.clarionsign.com
🚇 T-Centralen

Grand Hôtel £££

The traditional five-star hotel was opened in 1874 and has not lost any of its Belle-Époque charm. Here, people revel in more than a touch of luxury. Consequently,

the rich and beautiful, VIPs and Nobel Prize winners have been coming here for years to enjoy the exquisite cuisine and the breathtaking view of the Royal Palace.

⊞ 181 F4 ✉ Södra Blasieholmshamnen 8
☎ 08 6 79 35 60; www.grandhotel.se
🚇 Kungsträdgården 🚌 65

Hotel Diplomat £££

This pretty Art Nouveau house is located directly on Strandvägen, one of the most expensive addresses in Stockholm. Elegance and finesse continue inside, too, not only in the rooms, several of which have a sea view, but also in the collection of refined artworks.

⊞ 182 A4 ✉ Strandvägen 7C
☎ 08 4 59 68 00; www.diplomathotel.com
🚇 Kungsträdgården 🚌 47, 69, 76 🚊 7

Hotel Hellsten £££

Old building, new interior – describes this hotel in a nutshell. The 78 rooms reflect the style of Per Hellsten, who worked as a photographer for a long time in Africa and Asia. Many of the mementoes he brought back from his travels decorate the hotel, whereby his great love for ruby red really comes to the fore. It is worth taking a look at the suites. The Earth Bar has an exotic appeal, a bit like an ethnological museum and ranks among the hot spots of the Stockholm jazz scene. *Insider Tip*

⊞ 179 D2 ✉ Luntmakargatan 68
☎ 08 6 61 86 00; http://hellsten.se
🚇 Rådmansgatan

Hotel J £££

City tour and seaside holiday? Anyone staying here can have both. If you take the boat, you reach Nybrokajen or Slussen in 20 minutes, and on the bus it is just ten minutes. The design hotel displays a simple blue and white, maritime style. Most of the 45 rooms boast a balcony with

Finding Your Feet

a sea view. Summer house feeling is guaranteed. Its brasserie specialises in seafood, the preparation of which is inspired by New-England style cuisine.

➕ 183 west F1
✉ Ellensviksvägen 1, Nacka Strand
☎ 08 6 01 30 00; www.hotelj.se
🚌 443 C 🚢 From Nybrokajen and Slussen

Hotel Rival £££

A lifestyle hotel with modern furnishings of the finest kind in the trendy Södermalm district. The hotel shares its name with the inhouse cinema, in which concerts also take place. The owner is Benny Andersson from ABBA, so it is not surprising that the premiere of the film *Mamma Mia* was shown here. Anyone who has booked a room overlooking Mariatorget can lie back and relax in the bathtub and watch the people milling around in the square below. Those who like to lie in will be glad to hear that breakfast is served all day long.

➕ 181 D2 ✉ Mariatorget 3
☎ 08 54 57 89 00; www.rival.se
🚇 Mariatorget

Hotel Skeppsholmen ££

Designed by Nicodemus Tessin the Younger, this building once served as an army barracks and hospital, but this is no longer apparent. On the contrary, here guests stay in a design hotel with a winning combination of historical atmosphere and modern comforts. Quiet yet close to the town and with a fantastic panoramic view of the Royal Palace and the Old Town. The historic pavilion also belongs to the hotel.

➕ 182 B3 ✉ Gröna gången 1
☎ 08 4 07 23 00; www.hotelskeppsholmen.com
🚇 Kungsträdgården

Hotel Sven Vintappare ££

This establishment, built in 1607, exudes an enjoyable Gamla-Stan feeling, is in the heart of the bubbly Old Town and still manages to offer tranquil accommodation. Just seven rooms, all relatively small and decorated in country house style spread out over several floors. The bathrooms have Swedish marble and granite fittings, and look elegant.

➕ 181 E3 ✉ Sven Vintappares Gränd 3
☎ 08 22 41 40;
www.hotelsvenvintappare.se 🚇 Gamla Stan

Jumbo Stay £–££

A special kind of airport hotel: in a jumbo jet that once flew around the world. A 15-minute walk from Arlanda Airport, the airplane now serves as a youth hostel with multi-bed cabins for men or women. The double room in the cockpit provides a very special experience.

➕ 178 north A1 ✉ Jumbovägen 4
☎ 08 59 36 04 00; www.jumbohostel.se
🚇 Arlanda Express (bus and train)

Lady Hamilton Hotel ££–£££

The building in the heart of the Old Town dates back to the year 1470 and has been used as a hotel since 1975. Inside, the 34 rooms are a mix of Swedish country house style and old English country home. Awaiting guests in the basement of the Lady Hamilton is a "Relax Zone". The bubbling spring that has been in the hotel since it was built is now used as a plunge pool after the sauna. Those who like the Lady Hamilton will feel equally at home in the similarly conceived sister hotels, the Victory Hotel in Lilla Nygatan (no. 5) and the Lord Nelson Hotel in Västerlånggatan (no. 22), both in Gamla Stan.

➕ 181 E3 ✉ Storkyrkobrinken 5
☎ 08 50 64 01 00; www.thecollectorshotels.se
🚇 Gamla Stan

Långholmens Vandrarhem £

Regardless of whether guests check into the youth hostel or the hotel, they always land up in a former prison cell. Since 1975, heavyweight criminals are no longer incarcerated here, and have been replaced by tourists who are generally far more enthusiastic about their stay. The cells (= rooms) are all small; those who book the hotel rooms benefit from a bathroom, telephone and television; the youth hostel rooms are, however, very spartanly fitted. It is important to book well in advance.

🚩 180 west A3 ✉ Långholmsmuren 20
☎ 08 7 20 85 00; www.langholmen.com
🚇 Hornstull

Mälardrottningen ££

Barbara Hutton's white luxury motor yacht that was built in the 1920s has found its last anchorage just off Riddarholmen. Depending on how much guests want to spend, the choice of accommodation ranges from a simple cabin to the luxurious Owner's Cabin once used by Mrs Hutton. On view through the portholes is Stockholm's historic centre. The view from the restaurant on board is even more spectacular.

🚩 181 D3 ✉ Riddarholmen
☎ 08 54 51 87 80; www.malardrottningen.se
🚇 Gamla Stan

Nordic Light Hotel £££

The name of this hotel that has won numerous awards reveals its main theme. In the rooms, it is possible to select the colour of the lights to match individual mood. There is a skilful interplay of lights, regardless of whether in the lobby, Light Bar or lounge. In the winter light therapy packages and light boxes help to combat emerging depressions.

🚩 181 D4 ✉ Vasaplan 7
☎ 08 50 56 30 00; www.nordiclighthotel.com
🚇 T-Centralen

Scandic Gamla Stan ££

Built in the 17th century and furnished in Gustavian style, the Scandic even manages to keep pace with the nostalgic atmosphere of Gamla Stan. The 52 rooms have three-star comfort, which is definitely well above average.

🚩 181 E3 ✉ Lilla Nygatan 25
☎ 08 7 23 72 50; www.scandichotels.se
🚇 Gamla Stan

Scandic Grand Central ££–£££

Large, centrally located hotel. Housed in the former, 130-year-old "Lundberg Palace", the hotel has not sacrificed any of the residence's former charm. The 391 rooms make an elegant impression; the restaurant, bistro, bar and fitness studio cater to the well-being of the guests. Stockholmers also pop in to listen to the live music played here several times a week.

🚩 181 D5 ✉ Kungsgatan 70
☎ 08 51 25 20 00; www.scandichotels.com
🚇 T-Centralen

STF Gärdet £

Anyone expecting a youth hostel will be pleasantly surprised that this hostel offers single, double and family rooms, and that these also come with a TV, shower and WC. It is not even necessary to bring along your own sheets. Even the interior furnishings, conceived by designers, are appealing. Those who don't mind being somewhat away from the centre by Gärdet harbour will get a lot for a little money here.

🚩 179 east F3
✉ Sandhamnsgatan 59, Ladugårdsgärdet
☎ 08 4 63 22 99;
www.svenskaturistforeningen.se/gardet
🚌 1, 72

Story Hotel ££

A modern hotel in every respect This encompassed everything from the successful design to the self check-in and check-out. It is only possible to book on the Internet However, it is not a ghost-run hotel, there is a concierge and service in the restaurant. The smaller the rooms, the more economical the price.

Finding Your Feet

🔲 182 B5 ✉ Riddargatan 6 ☎ 08 54 50 39 40; https://storyhotel.nitesoft.se 🚇 Östermalmstorg

Villa Källhagen ££

People staying here are right out in the middle of the countryside by the bay of Djurgårdsbrunnsviken with its own landing stage and view of the Nordiska museet. The 36 rooms are modern and spacious, the restaurant serves good food and in the summer you can naturally sit outside. This is the ideal address for those who would like to combine their city trip with a walk or a jog by the water.

🔲 183 E5 ✉ Djurgårdsbrunnsvägen 10 ☎ 08 6 65 03 00; http://kallhagen.se 🚌 69

Food and Drink

In old travel guides, Swedish food does not score well. However, this opinion has long since been rectified. Swedish cuisine has received international awards on a number of occasions. Whilst traditional Swedish cuisine is marked by its high-calorie, farmhouse-style cuisine, the young chefs at the stove try to convince their guests with quality and not quantity (➤ 29).

Going out to Eat

- In terms of **prices**, Swedish restaurants are in the top category, especially in the lower and middle segment.
- Since **alcoholic drinks** are subject to hefty taxes, a glass of wine or a beer can actually increase the bill in a noticeable way.

Insider Tip

- Those looking for a good, inexpensive meal generally do well at an Asian restaurant. Even the many lunch buffets on offer are surprisingly inexpensive. If you opt for the *dagens lunch* or *dagens rätt*, the special of the day, it is usually possible to choose something from the salad bar at no additional charge. In addition to salad, the bar has bread and butter and alcohol-free drinks and coffee.
- On the whole, **meal times** correspond to the customs in Central Europe. Food restaurants often close at 10pm or 11pm.
- The Swedish names for the meals are as follows: *Frukost* means breakfast; *lunch* is lunch and *middag* is dinner/supper.
- **Tips** in Sweden tend to be the exception and not the rule. Those very happy with the service should just round up the bill total.

Alcohol

- It is only possible to buy alcoholic drinks with **more than 3.5% vol.** in state-run off-licences, ***systembolaget*** (www.systembolaget.se; Mon–Fri 10am–6pm/7pm, Sat 10am–3pm). Centrally located are, for example, the shops in Drottninggatan (no. 22), Folkungagatan (no. 56 and no. 101), Klarabergsgatan (no. 62), Sveavägen (no. 66), Birger Jarlsgatan (no. 84) and in Hötorgshallen.
- The **minimum age** for buying alcohol is 20.

Restaurant Prices
for a main dish or drinks
£ below kr200   ££ kr200–kr350   £££ over kr350

Shopping

Stockholm may seem somewhat more expensive than other European capitals, but the choice it offers is amazing. Swedish design is world famous. The city is heaven for antique collectors.

Shopping Districts

■ The main shopping street (pedestrian zone) in Stockholm is **Drottninggatan**, on which there are two large department stores, lots of boutiques and an increasing number of souvenir shops. Its south-east extension is Västerlånggatan, which with a similar setup leads in to Gamla Stan.

■ Located on **Hamngatan** is the large NK (Nordiska Kompaniet) department store. Opened in 1915, this store is worth a visit just to admire the architecture. Gallerian in Hamngatan (no. 37) is Stockholm's largest shopping mall.

■ However the more exclusive products are in the shops in **Biblioteksgatan** and around Stureplan. The high-priced Sturegallerian presumptuously calls itself the "House of Lifestyle".

■ Equally popular for shopping are the stores in **Birger Jarlsgatan**, **Nybrogatan** and **Grev Turegatan.**

■ **Södermalm** is also becoming a strong favourite. In this area, people shop in Götgatan, Hornsgatan and Nytorgsgatan.

■ 200 years of peace equal 200 years without destruction – that has made Sweden, and Stockholm in particular, a mecca for antique connoisseurs. There are a lot of antique shops in Västerlånggatan, Österlånggatan and Köpmansgatan as well as in the Vasastaden **district**.

■ Shopping tourists should learn to recognise signs bearing the inscription *rea* (clearance sale), *extra-pris* (special offer) and *fynd* (bargain) – they point out the particularly **good offers**.

Insider Tip

Opening Times and Special Points

■ State-regulated **opening times are** unknown in Sweden: the shops and department stores in the centre of town are also open on Sundays. The opening times differ, generally Mon–Fri 10am–6pm/7pm, Sat 10am–4pm/6pm, Sun noon–5pm.

■ A special north European feature is the *nummerlapp*. When you enter a shop, you pull a **ticket with a number printed on it** from a small machine. Hanging somewhere in the room is a display panel showing the number which is currently being served. It is not until your own number appears that you go to the counter. You will mainly come across *Nummerlappar* in small shops, chemists, department stores and markets but also at information desks, banks and post offices.

Markets

■ In the **Södermalm** district, a whopping three markets take place at the weekend: The **Hornstulls marknad** is a classic flea market. On Sundays, from April till October, 10am–5pm, stalls sell antiques, art, books etc. Food stands make sure visitors do not go hungry (www.hornstullsmarknad.se).

■ From August to October, farmers from the surrounding areas sell their produce on Saturdays between 10am and 3pm at the **Farmers' Market in Katarina Bangata**.

Finding Your Feet

- During the winter period, Stockholmers prefer to shop under cover – at the indoor market in **Götgatan no. 36**, in which **Bruno's Vintage Market** takes place on Sunday afternoons. Here the main focus is on hip clothes from the past (www.vintagemarket.se).
- Stockholm boasts three **indoor markets**: Besides the well-known **Östermalms saluhall** at Östermlamstorg (www.ostermalmshallen.se, ➤ 65), it is also worth visiting **Söderhallarna** at Medborgarplatsen (www.soderhallarna.se, ➤ 137) and the Hötorgshallen (www.hotorgshallen.se, ➤ 57) on the square bearing the same name.

Payment

- Cashless **payments** are very common in Sweden. People pay even small amounts with their credit or debit card; in some places, money is not even accepted (e.g. at automatic fuel pumps, and also in some restaurants). Thus, anyone going to Sweden definitely needs to take along some "plastic money".
- All well-known credit and debit cards are accepted (Visa, Mastercard, Maestro etc.).
- The Swedes pay for some things with their mobile phones – but this is currently only possible with a Swedish SIM card.

Entertainment

One of the popular places to go out now is Stureplan. This is where you will find the rich and beautiful. "See and be seen" is an important part of the evening's entertainment. In the Södermalm district – and here mainly in SoFo (➤ 136) – things are less conservative and more relaxed. This is where Stockholm's largest pub district has established itself over the last few years. Detailed information about events and an event calendar are available on the Visit Stockholm page (www.visitstockholm.com) and on the page Totally Stockholm (http://totallystockholm.se).

Opera and Theatre
- The **Kungliga Operan** (➤ 66) and the **Dramaten** theatre (➤ 65) are the best establishments in their respective area in Sweden.
- It is worth attending a performance at **Drottningholms Slottsteater** (➤ 159) just to see the auditorium. In Europe's only Rococo theatre, the original stage machinery is still in use.

Annual Events
- The **Stockholm Marathon** at the beginning of June is one of the largest events of its kind. From Östermalm, the runners run twice around the city. The finishing line is in the Olympic Stadium (www.stockholm marathon.se).
- Around **Midsommar** (Midsummer's) Eve, people celebrate on Skansen for three days wearing national dress and accompanied by lots of folk music (www.skansen.se).
- **Stockholm Pride** at the end of July is the largest homosexual and lesbian festival in northern Europe. The highlight is a street parade with more than 100,000 spectators (www.stockholmpride.org).

Norrmalm, Kungsholmen & Östermalm

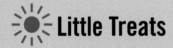 **Little Treats**

Take the Weight off Your Feet
Sit on the steps in front of **Stadshuset** (► 50) and dangle your feet in the water while you enjoy the view of Stockholm.

Theatre in the Park
In the summer, the **Parkteatern** (► 74) draws the crowds with its free performances in the city parks.

Little France in the Centre of Stockholm
Lap up the French lifestyle and still be able to enjoy *kanelbulle* – that is possible in **Petite France** (► 71).

Getting Your Bearings

Shopping, entertainment, museums and the sights – that is what most city tourists are looking for. These can all be found in the three city districts of Norrmalm, Kungsholmen and Östermalm, which together form the modern heart of Stockholm. However, they present visitors with difficult choices because there are lots of highlights.

Norrmalm is where the world of business and politics spends its working day, but culture has also found its niches there with the Opera and the Culture House. It is the modern part of the city where many high-rises were built between Sergels torg, Hötorget, Stureplan and Norrmalmstorg as part of a comprehensive redevelopment programme during the 1950s and 1960s. Nonetheless, outside the main business centre, there are still a fair number of historical buildings. In the Kungsträdgården, which the locals affectionately call *Kungsan*, the king used to grow his culinary herbs. These days, on warm summer days, the square can compete with every Italian piazza.

The right-angled street plan of Östermalm as well as the stately houses around the Östermalmstorg and on Strandvägen bear testimony to the time when Sweden was a major power. A particular highlight is the Strandvägen waterfront, with its Gründerzeit houses, which is regarded as one of Stockholm's top addresses. In this fitting setting is the Royal Dramatic Theatre with its richly decorated façade and the giant gilded sculptures by the entrance.

In the course of the last century, Kungsholmen has developed from an industrial and working-class district into one of the most popular – because it is not that expensive – residential areas in the city. Tourists, however, rarely venture further than the City Hall, the Swedish capital's landmark building.

Top 10
⭐ Stadshuset (City Hall) ➤ 50
⭐ Hagaparken (Haga Park) ➤ 54

Don't Miss
⓫ Hötorget ➤ 57
⓬ Nationalmuseet
   (National Museum) ➤ 59
⓭ Historiska museet
   (Swedish History Museum) ➤ 61

At Your Leisure

The Perfect Day

Perfect Days in...

Our itinerary takes you to the heart of this modern city. Begin the day with Stockholm's landmark building, then experience the contrast between the magnificent grand residences of the Founder Epoch and the rather austere post-war buildings. Some shopping and a museum visit also await you before you throw yourself into the city nightlife.

🕘 9:00am
Begin with the view from the ⭐ **City Hall** (➤ 50) tower over Stockholm and then go and see where the Nobel Prize winners celebrate.

🕥 10:30am
Walk to Gustav Adolfs torg, glance to the right at the Gamla Stan before proceeding to the **20 Royal Opera** (➤ 66), built in the spectacular Italian style of the Late Renaissance. Continue to the Kungsträdgården, where, when the weather is good, you can sit on a bench and watch the town slowly come to life. After a few hundred metres you stop off for your first bit of window shopping at the renowned department store of **Nordiska Kompaniet** (➤ 73). At **19 Sergels torg** (➤ 66) you will see the modern Stockholm and its functional buildings from the 1960s and 1970s. Time for a little coffee break? The **Kulturhuset** (➤ 66) offers enough opportunities to do that.

🕧 12:30pm
On Sveavägen you come to the **11 Hötorget** (➤ 57), one of the liveliest marketplaces in the town and to the neoclassical **Konserthuset** (➤ 57). Crossing Kungsgatan takes you to Stureplan and on to Östermalmstorg. Here, in the shops around the square, you can look out for the Swedish design articles and then drop in to **18 Östermalm Food Hall** (➤ 65; above) for lunch.

🕑 2:00pm
On the way to Nybroplan, make a quick visit to the **15 Army Museum** (➤ 63), the **16 Royal Stables** (➤ 64) or the Music Museum. Or march straight on to the **17 Royal Dramatic Theatre** (➤ 64), admire its spectacular façade and the gilded figures and then wander on to **Strandvägen** (➤ 63).

Getting Your Bearings

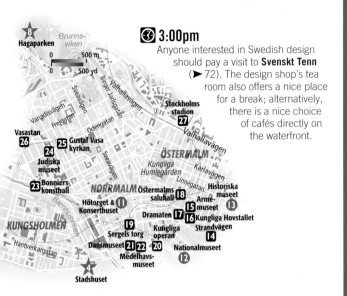

⏰ 3:00pm

Anyone interested in Swedish design should pay a visit to **Svenskt Tenn** (▶ 72). The design shop's tea room also offers a nice place for a break; alternatively, there is a nice choice of cafés directly on the waterfront.

⏰ 4:00pm

The ⑬ **Swedish History Museum** (▶ 61) gives you a comprehensive overview of Sweden's history.

⏰ 7:00pm

If you "only" want to stop off for a bite to eat, then **Prinsen** (▶ 71; below) with its classic interior and French-Swedish cuisine is a good choice. Those who like music or acrobatics to accompany their meal should opt for **Berns Bar & Bistro** (▶ 70) or **Wallmans Salonger** (▶ 74).

⏰ 10:00pm

A good option for night owls is Stureplan; here the **Sturecompaniet** (Sturegatan 4; www.sturecompagniet.se) – a former swimming pool and now a disco – is a good place to start the evening.

★ Stadshuset
(Stockholm City Hall)

Construction of the City Hall was one of the town's largest projects in the twentieth century. Today, it is one of the most widely visible landmarks in Stockholm, a building in which, quite profanely, the municipal authorities do their day-to-day work, but where also the annual Nobel Laureates are celebrated with great pomp and pageantry. Tours of the Stadshuset offer visitors a chance to view the most beautiful rooms.

The red-brick Stadshuset is located on the most south-easterly point of Kungsholmen Island on the banks of the Riddarfjärden. It would be hard to imagine a better location. The building with its 106m (348ft) high **tower** and the three golden crowns of Sweden's national coats of arms glittering at the top is visible for miles around and immediately seen by visitors arriving by train at the main station. The golden crowns are in memory of Tre Kronor (Three Crowns) Castle, once located on Stadsholmen Island, but which was destroyed during a fire in 1697 (Stockholm Palace now stands on this site; ▶ 80).

Art in the Park
Before going into the City Hall, it is worth taking a bit of time to look around the outside and visit the little park. At the foot of the tower, on the east side, under a canopy supported by columns is a **sculpture of the town founder Birger Jarl**. Standing on a column not far away from him, directly by the water, is the freedom fighter Engelbrekt Engelbrektsson. City Hall architect Ragnar Östberg commissioned the Swedish sculptor Carl Eldh to decorate the Stadshuspark with sculptures. Eldh opted for an ensemble of three famous people from the arts, an author (August Strindberg), poet (Gustav Fröding) and painter (Ernst Josephson). He received a lot of criticism for presenting them unclothed. Also naked are the two figures standing on the steps leading down to the water. *The Dance* is female and *The Song* is male, both of which are also by Carl Eldh. When the weather is good, Stockholmers like to go to the park and the terrace in front of the City Hall to enjoy the **view over Riddarfjärden** at Riddarholmen and Södermalm, browse a book or dangle their feet in the water.

View Over the City
A lift takes visitors up to the platform beneath the tower's belfry. The tower contains models and busts of people from the town's history, including the city patron Eric IX of Sweden, also called Eric the Saint. When visibility is good, the view over the town is the real spectacle: From this bird's-eye view, you clearly see Stockholm's island status

Insider Tip

and how the mainland, islands and water create a maze
of crooked channels through which the excursion boats
and skerry steamers plough back and forth. Riddarholmen
Island and the Old Town of Gamla Stan in particular seem
almost within reach.

Inspired by Venice

Stadshuset was based on the designs of **Ragnar Östberg**.
Building began in 1911. Twelve years later his main work,
inspired by the National Romantic style, Nordic Gothic
and Venetian palaces, was inaugurated. Similarities with
St Mark's Square in Venice are not coincidental. They
start with the position directly by the water, continue with
the arcades with their curved arches and culminate in the
Blue Hall and the Civic Courtyard.

**It is estimated
that about
eight million
red bricks
were used for
the Stadshuset**

The inauguration of the building was purposely planned
for Midsummer Night 1923. On that day exactly 400 years
earlier, on 23 June 1523, Gustav Vasa made his triumphant
entry into the Swedish capital. No other date since has
managed to embody Sweden's freedom better than this.

And even if the red-brick building does not quite attain the same elegance as the Venetian palaces, the Swedish population, according to a national survey, regard it as the most beautiful building in the country.

The Queen of Lake Mälar adorns the centre of a mosaic in the Golden Hall

A Building Full of Artworks

Behind the dark-red brick facade, grouped around two different-sized **courtyards**, are 250 offices and conference rooms for politicians and civil servants. The members of the Municipal Council meet in the Council Hall. What is more interesting for visitors, however, are the festival rooms with their attractive artworks, including mosaics, tapestries, paintings and statues in very different styles. Many artists took part in the interior furnishings, from artist Prince Eugen to the well-known furniture designer Carl Malmsten. There is a broad view over the city from the **Prince's Gallery**. Behind a row of columns is a fresco painted by Prince Eugen, *The City on the Water*.

Insider Tip

In Celebration of the Occasion

Every year on 10 December, the Stadshuset provides the venue for the banquet to honour the Nobel Prize Winners. Then, prizewinners, members of the royal family and festively dressed, hand-picked participants congregate in the **Blue Hall** for the festival banquet. Over 1,000 guests sit tightly packed together at the long tables and celebrate with the prizewinners. The king plays a rather minor role in the proceedings, which entails just one task: at the beginning of the meal he raises his glass and opens the banquet with the Swedish *skål* (cheers).

Surprisingly, you look in vain for the colour that gives its name to the hall. Originally, it was intended to paint the walls of the hall in a deep blue to symbolise the sea; the clinker bricks had already been painstakingly hewn by hand in wave form before the architect Ragnar Östberg changed his mind on the spur of a moment and left the walls in red.

After visiting the City Hall, the shore path along Riddarfjärden offers a pretty walk

After the banquet, the Nobel Laureates go off to the dance floor to the Golden Hall, which rightly deserves its name. The walls comprise of a golden puzzle with more than 18 million individual mosaic tiles. It took ten years to implement this design by **Einar Forseth**, which was inspired by Byzantine art. Enthroned at the head of the Hall is the *Queen of Lake Mälar*, the mediator between East and West. The goggle-eyed goddess with protruding plaits was originally seen as a very controversial artwork.

TAKING A BREAK

Ragnars Skafferi in Stadshuset is open from Mon–Fri 7:30am–4pm. In addition to snacks, it serves good and in-expensive lunches that include bread and butter, salad, coffee or tea, between 11am and 2pm

➕ 180 C4 ✉ Hantverkargatan 1 ☎ 08 50 82 90 58; http://international.stockholm.se/the-city-hall ⏰ Stadshuset: Tours June–Aug daily 9am–4pm every half an hour; also open the rest of the year but with fewer tours; tower: June–Aug daily 9:10am–5:10pm, May, Sep 9:10am–3:50pm 🚇 T-Centralen G3 💰 kr70–kr100

INSIDER INFO

■ From Stadshuset/Stadshusparken follow the **shore path** that runs parallel to the road Norr Mälarstrand. Moored along the waterfront are many historical boats. Info panels provide information about the history of these veterans. What is more, there is a wonderful view over the Riddarfjärden to Gamla Stan, Södermalm and Långholmen.

■ **Norr Mälarstrand House (no. 66)** was the home of adventurer and writer Sven Hedin from 1935 until his death in 1952. He came to fame abroad predominantly for his three books *Transhimalaya*, *From Pole to Pole* and *Riddles of the Gobi Desert*.

■ At the end of Norr Mälarstrand, you reach **Rålambshovsparken**. The lawns invite you to relax, sunbathe, play boules and picnic. If you are lucky, you may catch one of the regular summer performances by the Parkteatern in the amphitheatre (➤74).

■ Just a bit farther along and you come to **Smedsuddsbadet,** a bathing area with a small sandy beach (the distance from the City Hall to the beach is about 2km/1.2mi).

⭐⑧Hagaparken
(Haga Park)

The lawns of the vast park on the west bank of Brunsviken Lake are an attractive place to have a picnic, and the Stockholmers use the paths for jogging and cycling. Since her marriage, Crown Princess Victoria and Prince Daniel have lived in Haga Palace. The other buildings, including Gustav III's Pavilion and the Copper Tents, are open to the public.

Gustav III had great plans for the Haga premises north of the town area by Brunsviken, his aim being no less than to create a second Versailles here. Yet, after his murder in

1792 at a masked ball, his dream palace was left unfinished. Today, all that remains of the building are the overgrown foundations, which have been used on many occasions as the backdrop for film and theatre productions. In the Park Museum is a model that provides an idea of what the palace was supposed to look like.

During Gustav's lifetime, the "only" part that was completed was the palace park, an English landscape garden, for which more than 20,000 trees were planted. In the mid-19th century, the park was then opened to the general public. Since then, it has enjoyed great popularity with the Stockholmers who sunbathe and barbecue on the broad lawns in the summer and toboggan down the slopes in the winter.

Haga Palace, the new home of the Swedish Crown Princess Victoria and her husband Prince Daniel

Haga Palace

The relatively unostentatious palace was built at the beginning of the 19th century in the Italian Palazzo style for Gustav IV Adolf. It was also in these apartments that the present King Carl XVI Gustav spent his early years with his siblings until they moved into the Royal Palace in 1947. Subsequently, Haga Palace was used to accommodate guests on state visits. It was not until 2009 that the Swedish government decided to turn over the residence to Crown Princess Victoria and her future husband. The palace was comprehensively renovated and a year later the newly-weds moved into the home befitting their social status.

Gustav III Pavilion

The Gustav III Pavilion was started in 1787 and built according to the plans of Olof Tempelmann. Luis Masreliez was put in charge of the interior furnishings. As with the large Haga Palace, Gustav III was also involved in the planning and building process, drew sketches and extended among other things both wings of the building with window axes.

Today, the pavilion is regarded as one of the most beautiful examples of the Gustavian style, whereby it is mainly the interior with its **wall paintings** and **halls of mirrors** that really elicit admiration. Various alterations were made after Gustav's death. These were not reversed until Masreliez's original drawings were found by chance.

The Copper Tents

The three **Koppartälten** (Copper Tents), which architect Jean Desprez based on the military tents of the Roman army, look very exotic. They once served as stables, today they house a restaurant and a museum dedicated to the history of the park. In 1953, the middle tent was destroyed by fire, but was faithfully rebuilt under the management of Ragnar from 1962 to 1964.

The Burial Island

Located on a small island in Haga Park is the **Kungliga begravningsplatsen** (Royal Cemetery), in which numerous members of the royal family have found their last resting place, including King Gustav IV Adolf who died in 1973.

Further Attractions

Exotic birds and butterflies flutter around in the various greenhouses of the 🔢 **Fjärils- & Fågelhuset (The Butterfly House)** not far from the Copper Tents. Other sights include the **Ekotemplet (Echo Temple)**, which was originally intended as an airy dining room for Gustav III, the Chinese pagoda, the Turkish kiosk, the Finnish huts and the cavalry supply farm now used as a hotel (www. stallmastaregarden.se).

Although the **Café Vasaslätten** is only open in summer and
when the sun is shining, it offers a beautiful view of the lake
One of its specialities is *hagabulle*, a delicious cinnamon
bun – which is naturally homemade. An alternative for
lunch, especially when the weather is not as nice, is the
Wärdshus Koppartälten in one of the two Copper Tents.

A popular
place to go
even in winter:
Haga Park
and the
Copper Tents

➕ 178 A/B5 ✉ Uppsalavägen, Solna 🚇 Odenplan, the Bus 515

Gustav III's Pavilion
☎ 08 4 02 61 30
🕐 June–Aug Tue–Sun tours (45 min.) 3pm 💰 kr100

Haga Park Museum
☎ 08 27 42 52 🕐 Mid-May–end Sep daily 11am–5pm,
otherwise Fri–Sun 10am–3pm 💰 Free

Butterfly (and Bird) House
☎ 08 7 30 39 81; www.fjarilshuset.se
🕐 April–Sep daily 10am–5pm 💰 kr155

Royal Cemetery
🕐 May–Aug Thu 1pm–3pm

INSIDER INFO

- Haga Park is a good starting point for a number of other excursions: On the other
bank of Brunsviken Lake is the **Bergianska botaniska trädgården** (Bergius Botanic
Garden), a large botanical garden with tropical and Mediterranean greenhouses
(➕ 178 northbound. C5; Gustafsborgsvägen 4; tel: 08 16 37 01; www.bergianska.se;
April–Sep daily 11am–5pm, otherwise Mon–Fri 11am–4pm, Sat, Sun until 5pm;
metro to Universitetet; admission kr80).

- To the south of Haga Park is the **Norra begravningsplatsen** (**North Cemetery**), one of
Sweden's largest and most beautiful cemeteries. Many architects contributed to the
work extending the cemetery, among them Gunnar Asplund. Numerous well-known
artists such as Carl Eldh and Carl Milles designed the tombs and sculptures. The list
of prominent people buried here is long. It includes among others: Ingrid Bergman,
Alfred Nobel, August Strindberg and Charlotte Wahlström (Solna Kyrkväg, Grind 3;
http://norrabegravningsplatsen.se; Bus 3, 59, 77).

⑪ Hötorget ("Haymarket")

If you walk a good 250m (820ft) north along Sergelgatan, the little street running from Sergels torg, you will come to the market on Hötorget Square. Countless generations of farmers from the surrounding area have come here to sell their products, and to this day the square still provides the venue for regular weekly markets. On the east side of the square is the neoclassical Stockholm Concert Hall.

Hay was traded on the square until 1856 – hence the name Hötorget which means "Haymarket". Later, the sales of wood, hay and straw were moved to Norrmalmstorg. The **Hötorgshallen** (Haymarket Market Hall) was set up from 1880, in which to this day you can buy fruit and vegetables, fish and meat, sausage and cheese. Until 1914 when livestock trading was transferred to the market at the main station, buyers could even buy beef, pork and mutton at the Hötorget. The fruit, vegetable, flower and clothing stands at Hötorgot have survived all the changes.

In the 1910s and 1920s, two striking buildings appeared on Hötorget Square, the **PUB** department store, where Greta Garbo once used to work as a milliner – and the concert hall. In subsequent years, too, the redevelopment of Stockholm's city centre did not stop at Hötorget. Its southern section has undergone significant changes. The five skyscrapers **Hötorgsskraporna** are particularly eye-catching, if not quite to everyone's taste.

Konserthuset

View of Hötorget and the Stockholm Concert Hall

Built in 1924 based on the design of Iva Tengborn, the Stockholm Concert Hall is regarded as one of the most important neoclassical buildings in Sweden. The blue facade and the high grey granite columns, which come from the quarry of Vånevik north of Kalmar, are particularly

Norrmalm, Kungsholmen & Östermalm

A MURDER APPALS SWEDEN
On 28 February 1986, Olof Palme, the then prime minster of Sweden was murdered on the Sveavägen/Tunnelgatan crossing. Just before that, Palme – as was usual at the time – was out and about without a security guard, and had just been to the Grand cinema in Sveavägen (no. 45). The circumstances surrounding the crime have never been clarified and the murderer was never caught. The Tunnelgatan, just a few hundred metres to the north of Hötorget was renamed Olof Palmes gata, a plaque in the pavement commemorates the politician.

striking. It is possible to go round the rooms and admire the interior design – except during concerts – even during the annual awards of the Nobel Prizes on 10 December. Otherwise it is here that the **Royal Stockholm Philharmonic** plays, an orchestra which regularly welcomes guest musicians. In front of the concert house is the **Orfeus fountain**, a work by sculptor Carl Milles.

TAKING A BREAK

The fast food restaurant **Kajsas Fisk** has not been an insider tip for the Stockholmers for a long time. It has been serving fresh fish in the basement of the Hötorgshalle for 30 years for an almost unbeatable price. The atmosphere of a market hall does not exactly invite one to linger, but the salmon, cod and plaice – and of course the fish soup – are worth every single krona.

Flea market on Hötorget; in the background, the PUB department store from 1916

➕ 179 D1 ✉ Hötorget ☎ 08 20 72 62; http://kajsasfisk.se
🕐 Mon–Thu 11am–6pm, Fri 11am–7pm, Sat 11am–4pm 🚇 Hötorget, G1, 55, 57

Konserthuset
➕ 179 D1 ✉ Hötorget 8 ☎ 08 50 66 77 88; www.konserthuset.se
🕐 Mon–Fri 11am–5pm, Sat 11am–3pm and in each case 2 hours before the respective concert 🚇 Hötorget 🚌 1, 55, 57

Hötorgshallen (Hörtorget Food Hall)
➕ 179 D1 ✉ Hötorget; www.hotorgshallen.se
🕐 Mon–Thu 10am–6pm, Fri 10am–7pm, Sat 10am–4pm

INSIDER INFO

- The Hötorget is a meeting place for film friends because the **Filmstaden Sergel** (www.sf.se) has 14 screens showing the latest blockbusters.
- The **Hötorget metro station** has been upgraded with various artworks. The Swedish-Danish artist Gun Gordillos installed more than 100 strips of white neon light which, in combination with the light green tiles on the walls, bathe the station in a surreal light (▶ 26).

⑫ Nationalmuseet
(National Museum)

The National Museum in the south of Blasieholmen is not only Sweden's most important art museum with around 700,000 exhibits, it is also a city landmark in its own right. Due to extensive renovation work however, art lovers will have to wait until 2018 until they can again view the exhibition in its full glory.

This impressive building based on the plans of Friedrich August Stüler, who also designed the New Museum in Berlin, was built in the mid-19th century. Probably due to the beautiful location directly on Strömmen Bay, Stüler was inspired to create a building in the **Italian neo-Renaissance style**.

Stockholm's National Museum is a palace of fine arts, both inside and out

The collections focus on 18th and 19th century Swedish painting. Two of the most famous paintings adorn the huge **flight of stairs** leading up to the galleries: *The Entry of King Gusta Vasa of Sweden into Stockholm*, 1523 and *Midwinter's Sacrifice* by Carl Larsson (1853–1919). The latter, though always intended for this space, was not hung here until 1997 after a long odyssey through other locations.

Also particularly worth seeing is the excellent **French Collection,** which includes works by Cézanne, Degas, Gauguin, Manet and Monet. Works by Rembrandt are also on show of course. His most important work in the Stockholm collection is *The Conspiracy of Claudius Civilis*. It depicts the chieftain of a Celtic clan living in what we now know as the Netherlands during the time of Emperor Augustus and the Revolt of the Batavi, an uprising against the Roman Empire.

Besides the many paintings, sculptures, drawings and graphics, the museum also has a comprehensive **Design and Applied Arts Collection** which provides an overview of Swedish crafts and design up to the 21st century.

TAKING A BREAK

Anyone near the National Museum who fancies some high-quality fish for lunch should head for the acclaimed star restaurant **Wedholms Fisk** (**£££**; Nybrokajen 17; tel: 08 6 11 78 74; www.wedholmsfisk.se; Mon–Fri 11:30am–2pm and 6pm–11pm, Tue–Fri 11:30am–11pm, Sat 5pm–11pm), which ranks as one of the best fish restaurants in the town. The lunch menu is not much more expensive than at other restaurants and is a perfect way to convince yourself of the quality of the main dishes.

RENOVATION TILL 2018

The National Museum is currently closed to the public; it has been undergoing renovation work since 2013, and this is likely to continue until 2018. In order to ensure that visitors to Stockholm do not have to miss the collections completely, some of the exhibits are on view in the **Konstakademien** and in the Kulturhuset **Stadsteatern**. Since these alternative sites are much smaller than the National Museum, the selection of works on show is very restricted. Information regarding ongoing exhibitions is available on the website of the National Museum.

Larsson's *Midwinter Sacrifice* depicts the sacrifice of the legendary Swedish king Domalde after a series of bad harvests

---

Nationalmuseet
🚋 181 F4 ✉ Södra Blasieholmen
☎ 08 51 95 43 00; www.nationalmuseum.se
🕐 closed until probably 2018 🚇 Kungsträdgården

Konstakademien
🚋 181 D/E4 ✉ Fredsgatan 12 🕐 Tue, Thu 10am–8pm, Wed, Fri–Sun 10am–5pm
🚇 T-Centralen, Kungsträdgården 🎫 Free

Kulturhuset Stadsteatern
🚋 181 E4 ✉ Sergels torg 🕐 Mon–Fri 11am–7pm, Sat, Sun 11am–5pm
🚇 T-Centralen, Kungsträdgården 🎫 Free

INSIDER INFO

- Fans of modern and contemporary art should definitely make a visit to the nearby **Moderna Museet** (► 117) on Skeppsholmen.
- There is a nice **walk** from the National Museum to the green and tranquil islands of Skeppsholmen and Kastellholmen (► 126).

⑬ Historiska Museet
(Swedish History Museum)

The Swedish History Museum in Stockholm, like the institutions in Oslo, Copenhagen and Haithabu, boasts one of the largest collections on the Viking and Nordic Iron Age periods. The showrooms, which follow a modern didactic museum approach, also include exhibits from other cultural eras such as the Romanesque, Gothic, Reformation and Baroque periods.

STATE PROPERTY
A Swedish law stipulates that any art objects made of gold, silver or copper alloys that are more than 100 years old will be bought by the state. This means that an unusually large amount of precious antiques have been preserved for posterity.

Insider Tip

Although one generally tends to save the best until last, it is perhaps better in the Swedish History Museum to start with the highlight – the **Guldrummet (Gold Room)** – since the museum collections are so diverse and comprehensive that you may otherwise not have the time or energy to appreciate it properly. The circular, darkened room in the arched cellar gives the impression of a large walk-in bank vault and is similarly protected with steel concrete walls. After all, the vault contains 52kg (115lb) of gold and more than 200kg (440lb) of silver. Waiting to be admired in the glass showcases are precious art objects from long-forgotten times. Goldsmithing work from the Migration Period, silver chains from the Viking period, goblets and reliquaries from the Middle Ages.

1,000 years of Swedish history

Armbands from the Viking period adorned with ornaments

A central section of the museum is dedicated to the history from the 11th century – in other words long before Sweden existed as a country – to the present day. A timeline leads visitors through the centuries, whereby new and surprising perspectives constantly open up. Worth noting is that the history of the Sami is recounted from their perspective.

Norrmalm, Kungsholmen & Östermalm

The Vikings

For a very long time, people
believed the stories of marauding
and plundering men with red
beards who, in their fast, slim
boats, provoked fear and terror
throughout Europe. Today, we
know that the majority of the
Vikings were not warriors, but
farmers, traders and craftsmen
and that only a small number of
them actually set off to plunder.
The Viking section of the Swedish
History Museum, which with
around **4,000 artefacts** is one of
the largest in the world, supports
this corrected picture of them
with everyday objects and insights
into their daily lives. In Lake Mälar,
around 30km (19mi) to the west
of Stockholm, is the little birch
island with the **Birka** Viking settle-

This altar with
scenes from
the life of
Saint Birgitta
dates back to
the 15th
century

ment, which in the meantime is listed as a UNESCO World
Heritage site. The Historiska museet also contains a model
of the entire town to illustrate the daily life of the many
peace-loving Vikings.

And what else is there to see? A lot! The top floor is
dedicated to the **Middle Ages** and **church art.** One of
the most valuable pieces is the gilded wooden figure of
Maria from Viklau from the early Middle Ages. And in the
prehistoric collections, visitors are led through different
time periods using eight life stories.

TAKING A BREAK

In the museum restaurant **Café Rosengården**, besides
snacks, you can also order from the inexpensive lunch
menu between 11:30am and 2pm. In the summer, it is
possible to sit outside.

➕ 182 B5 ✉ Narvavägen 13–17
☎ 08 51 95 56 00; www.historiska.se
🕐 June–Aug daily 11am–6pm, Sep Thu–Tue 11am–6pm, Wed until 8pm,
otherwise Tue–Fri noon–6pm, Sat, Sun 11am–6pm
🚇 Östermalmstorg G44, 56, 69, 76 🚌 7
💰 Free

INSIDER INFO

- At the reception, you can ask for an **audio guide** (kr30), which will guide you through
  the prehistoric, Viking and Gold Hall collections. The audio guide for smart phones
  costs kr15.
- In the **museum shop,** you will find very readable books on the history of Stockholm.

At Your Leisure

14 Strandvägen

The good 1km (0.6mi) long Strandvägen stretches from Nybroplan in the west to the other side of Djurgårdsbron in the east. Until the end of the 19th century, this was a disreputable harbour district. During the **Stockholm Exhibition in 1897**, Stockholm's new grand boulevard was, after an extensive period of construction, finally inaugurated. And the better road led to the improvement of the houses. Well-known architects erected veritable palaces, which were soon inhabited by the wealthy Stockholmers. To this day, little has changed in this row of houses by the water, so it is not very surprising that a lot of prominent people live here and that there are many exclusive shops on the ground floors. Especially in the afternoon, the fine facades really gleam in the sunlight. That is when it is particularly fun to wander across the Strandvägen with its three rows of lime trees and enjoy the view of Djurgården, Blasieholmen and Skeppsholmen. Bobbing up and down by the quay are modern and historical boats which give the boulevard a certain maritime flair. On the other side of Djurgårdsbron is the small **Nobelparken** in which you can find almost every tree that is native to Sweden.

🚻 182 A–C3 🚌 69, 76 🚊 7

Insider Tip

15 Armémuseet (Army Museum)

The museum buildings were built in the 17th century as an arsenal for the production and storage of weapons. Now, it portrays **Sweden's military history** from the Vikings to the present day. Exhibits include banners and other trophies captured in war as well as figures of soldiers in various uniforms. Important battles of the Swedish

Since 1897, Strandvägen, with its magnificent buildings, has been the city's favourite promenade

army are reconstructed, and in the **saddle room** visitors can see what role horses played in battle The **Raoul Wallenberg Room** commemorates the Swedish diplomat who, in Budapest in 1944, saved at least 20,000 Jews from being deported to Auschwitz, but was deported himself to the Soviet Union where he eventually died in prison.

✚ 182 A5 ✉ Riddargatan 13
☎ 08 51 95 63 01; www.sfhm.se
🕑 June–Aug daily 10am–5pm, otherwise Tue 11am–8pm, Wed–Sun 11am–5pm
🚊 13, 14 💰 Free

16 Kungliga hovstallet (Royal Stables)

The history of the Royal Stables stretches back to 1535 and King Gustav Vasa. These days, only 20 horses are kept in the stables. They are used for the public appearances of the royal family and pull one of the **50 glamorous carriages.** It is possible to see these carriages on a museum tour. A highlight is a state coach clad with glass that was already being used in 1897 during the reign of Oscar II. Visitors can also admire a fleet of around **20 state cars,** including a Cadillac from 1969 and a Mercedes from 1950. Although the Mercedes is the oldest car in the fleet it is still used from time to time. For instance, on her wedding day, Crown Princess Victoria drove this car to Storkyrkan.

✚ 182 A5 ✉ Väpnargatan 1
☎ 08 4 02 61 06; www.kungahuset.se/hovstallet
🕑 Visits only with tours, mid-June until mid-Aug Mon–Fri 1pm and 3pm, otherwise Sat 1pm (each time in English)
🚇 Östermalms torg, Kungsträdgården
🚌 2, 55 🚊 13, 14 💰 kr100

The Dramaten built in the Viennese Art Nouveau style presides over the lively Nybroplan Square

A visit in Östermalms saluhall – a feast for the palate, eyes and nose

17 Dramaten
(Royal Dramatic Theatre)

Thanks to generous funding by the lottery, architect Fredrik Liljekvist was able to get many well-known artists involved in his theatre project. The eye-catcher is the richly ornamented facade of white Ekeberg marble; its lavish shapes are reminiscent of the Art Nouveau in Vienna. Since it opened in 1908 with Strindberg's play *Master Olof*, the impressive building on Nybroplan has been Sweden's National Theatre. Besides the facade, on either side of the entrance there are two gilded figures: *Drama* and *Poetry* by John Börjesson that also demand attention as do two further sculptures *Tragedy* and *Comedy* in the foyer. The splendour continues inside; sculptures and busts adorn the marble foyer, the auditorium radiates in red and gold.

Ingmar Bergman, the director who became world famous first and foremost for his films was the director of the Royal Dramatic Theatre from 1963–1966. The stage has seen great actors such as Max von Sydow, Greta Garbo and Bibi Andersson. A life-size statue a few paces away from the entrance towards Birger Jarlsgatan is of one of the most popular Swedish actresses in the 20th century, Margaretha Krook.

It is also just a short walk to the small **Berzelii Parken (Berzelius Park)**, which takes its name from the doctor and chemist Berzelius (1779–1848).

🔲 182 A5 ✉ Nybroplan 2
☎ 08 6 67 06 80; www.dramaten.se
🎭 Tour Sat 5pm 🚇 Kungsträdgården, Östermalmstorg 🚃 2, 55 🎟 kr60

18 Östermalms saluhall
(Östermalm Food Hall)

Written in golden letters on the facade of this listed red-brick facade is the word "Saluhall": market hall. In 1888, it was ceremoniously opened by King Oscar II and has remained a top address for connoisseurs ever since. However, before getting down to some serious spending, it is worth taking a closer look at the carved wooden stalls, many of which have been in the same family for generations. You will probably have to go without this treat until about 2018 though. Östermalms saluhall is in the process of being renovated; market trading is currently taking place in a temporary market hall at Östemalmstorg.

Insider Tip

In 2007 Östermalms saluhall was elected one of the ten best food halls in the world. Star chef Jamie Oliver also sings its praises highly. Delicatessen as far as the eye can see. Fruit and vegetables, fresh fish, elk and reindeer steaks, salami from Italy, Swiss cheese, coffee, tea and spices from all over the world.

Anyone who comes at lunchtime can eat their lunch standing at a table and enjoy a culinary world tour in the process.

Östermalmstorg in front of the market hall is a popular meeting place. The square's controversial group of two modern sculptures, *The Meeting* by Willy Gordon, shows a man exposing himself and carrying a piece of meat on his shoulder looking down on a recumbent woman.

🚪 182 A5 ✉ Östermalmstorg 1
☎ www.ostermalmshallen.se
🕐 Mon–Fri 9:30am–7pm, Sat 9:30am–6pm
🚇 Östermalmstorg

🔟 Sergels torg (Sergel's Square)

The redesign of the centre of Stockholm began in the 1950s. Around half of the old residences were torn down and replaced with new buildings. They were followed by Sergels torg in 1960, named after the sculptor Johan Tobias Sergel. The square has a lower level for pedestrians with black and white tiles, often less respectfully referred to by the locals as the *Plattan* (the "Slab"), and 10m (33ft) above it another level for the cars.

A notable feature of the square is its roundabout in the shape of a super ellipse. Rising up in the middle is a 37m (121ft) high, glass obelisk, which is lit at night. Also a real eye-catcher are the five identical-looking 19-storey buildings on the north side of the

square, the **Five Trumpet Blasts**, which were designed by well-known Swedish architects.

Without a doubt, Sergels torg is one of the most important squares in the Swedish capital. This is where political demonstrations take place; this is where people come to celebrate en masse. When the Swedish ice-hockey team scores another victory, their fans have been known to dance in the fountain around the foot of the glass obelisk.

To the south of the Sergels torg is the **Kulturhuset (Culture House)**, a functional, rather austere building with a glass facade that was built in 1974. For the people of Stockholm, this "glass palace of culture" is a bit like a living room. There are places to sit all over the building; in the reading room, people can read daily newspapers from all over the world, and the chess tables are usually in use from first thing in the morning. Three art galleries regularly organise free exhibitions; cafés and restaurants serve reasonably priced meals. The **Stadsteatern (City Theatre)** has also moved into the Culture House. To ensure that culture remains affordable for everyone, besides the evening performances, there are also matinees for which the tickets are not as expensive. At lunchtime, the "Soup Theatre" performs little plays – food is delivered with the entertainment.

🚪 181 E5 ✉ Sergels torg 3
☎ 08 50 62 02 12; www.kulturhuset.stockholm.se
🕐 Tickets and information Mon–Fri 9am–7pm, Sat, Sun 11am–5pm
🚇 Hötorget, Centralen 🚌 54, 57, 69, 91

🔟 Kungliga operan (Royal Opera)

The magnificent opera house in late Renaissance style was designed by the Swedish architect Alex Anderberg and inaugurated in 1898. Anderberg designed the opera to match the palace complex

Sergels torg – the modern heart of the Swedish capital

The Royal Opera's interior also has its fair share of opulent embellishments

on the other side of the river. The previous building dates back to **King Gustav III** (1746–1792), who had the first opera house built on this location. In 1792, aristocratic conspiracy culminated in the assassination of the patron of the arts during a masked ball in "his" opera. The idea for Giuseppe Verdi's opera *A Masked Ball* was based on this incident.

The Royal ballet is also part of the ensemble, and the Royal Orchestra, founded in 1526, is one of the oldest in the world. All of Sweden's famous singers, from Jenny Lind to Gösta Winbergh, have sung in the opera house.

🚩 181 E4   ✉ Gustav Adolfs torg
☎ 08 7 91 44 00; www.operan.se
🕐 ticket sales Mon–Fri 3pm–6pm,
Sat noon–3pm   🚇 Kungsträdgården

㉑ Dansmuseet (Dance Museum)

Opened in 1999 in a former bank building on Gustav Adolfs torg, the Dance Museum highlights all aspects of the visual and performing arts. The comprehensive collection was put together by the aristocrat and art collector Rolf de Maré, who initiated the famous Ballets Suédois in 1920, which successfully toured Europe and the USA for five years. The exhibition shows costumes, masks, set designs, photographs and posters from all over the world, including African dance masks,

Russian ballet costumes, Indian demons but also the Swedish national dress worn at midsummer.

🚩 181 E4   ✉ Drottninggatan 17
☎ 08 4 41 76 51; www.dansmuseet.se
🕐 Tue–Fri 11am–5pm, Sat, Sun noon–4pm
🚇 Kungsträdgården, T-Centralen   🖐 Free

㉒ Medelhavsmuseet (Mediterranean Museum)

On show in the museum are art treasures from the Mediterranean and Near East, ranging from Egypt to Greece and the Roman Empire. Of particular interest is the collection of ancient Cypriot art, including a group of terracotta figures that archaeologists found in the 1930s. The Goldrummet (Gold Room) contains valuable gold objects found in the Mediterranean area. Bagdad Café, the museum restaurant, focuses on Mediterranean dishes. Its lunch menu is popular and reasonably priced.

Insider Tip

The Observatorielunden Park with its striking Public Library

🏛 181 E4 ✉ Fredsgatan 2; www.varlds
kulturmuseerna.se/medelhavsmuseet
🕐 Tue–Fri noon–8pm, Sat noon–5pm
🚇 Kungsträdgården, T-Centralen
🚌 3, 52, 62, 65 💶 Free

🖼 Bonniers Konsthall

The exhibitions at Bonniers
Konsthall generally feature up-and-
coming artists. A foundation also
gives grants to the young artists.
The five-floor building not only has
an eye-catching glass facade, its
original shape is reminiscent of an
iron or an asymmetric arrow.
🏛 178 B1 ✉ Torsgatan 19
☎ 08 7 36 42 48; www.bonnierskonsthall.se
🕐 Wed noon–8pm, Thu–Sun noon–5pm
🚇 St. Eriksplan 🚌 3, 4, 70, 72, 77 💶 Free

🖼 Judiska museet (Jewish Museum)

In the second half of the 18th century, there are the first records of
migrant Jews arriving in Stockholm
and practising their religion. Today
about 20,000 people of Jewish faith
live in Sweden, half of them in
greater Stockholm.
The museum tells the
story of Swedish Jews,
their religion and the
Holocaust. Among the
most important exhibits
are a Torah, a wedding
canopy and a
collection of
Menorah (seven-
armed candelabra).
🏛 178 B2

✉ Hälsingegatan 2 ☎ 08 55 77 35 60;
www.judiska-museet.se 🕐 The museum is
currently closed for renovation until 2018
🚇 Odenplan, St. Eriksplan
🚌 4, 50, 61, 67, 69, 72, 73 💶 kr80

🖼 Gustaf Vasa kyrka (Gustaf Vasa Church)

This church by architect August
Lindegren has the ground plan of a
Greek cross, was built in the neo-
Baroque style based on the model
of Italian churches and consecrated
in 1906. With pews capable of sitting around 1,200 people beneath
the 60m (167ft) high dome, Gustaf
Vasa kyrka – named after the first
Swedish king after the Kalmar
Union – ranks as one of the largest
churches in Stockholm. It is famous
for its **main altar**, dating back to
1731 by court sculptor Burchard
Precht, which was originally made
for the Uppsala Cathedral. At the
end of the 19th century, the munic-
ipality bought the valuable artwork
and integrated it into the new Gustaf
Vasa kyrka. Beneath the central
section is a three-aisled crypt that
originally served as a burial church
and was later extended into
a columbarium that has
space for 35,000 urns.

🏛 178 C2
✉ Karlsbergvägen 5
🕐 Mon–Thu 11am–6,
Fri–Sun 11–3
🚇 Odenplan
🚌 2, 4, 40, 42,
47, 53

26 Vasastan

In the 18th century, as part of the extension of the town, the first houses were built in Vasastan, the north part of Normalm. The district received its name from Vasagatan Street which leads north from the centre, although in actual fact if you follow the Drottninggatan or Sveavägen Streets north, you also come to Vasastan after crossing the Tegnérgatan Square. It is home to two of the most beautiful parks in the city.

Vasaparken was laid out at the beginning of the 20th century as a green lung for the city. It has broad lawns and most of the trees in the park date back to this period. Children's book author Astrid Lindgren lived for 60 years at no. 46 Dalagatan Street overlooking the park; in 2006, the **Astrid Lindgrens terrass** was inaugurated in her honour on the east side of the park.

In the **Observatorielunden** Park, high above Sveavägen Street, you will find the observatory, built by Carl Harleman, and also the impressive looking **public library**. The latter was completed in 1927 and is one of Gunnar Asplund's first functionalist works. In the cylinder-shaped main room of the library, the bookshelves reach up to the ceiling.

➕ 178 A3–C2 🚇 Odenplan

27 Stockholms stadion (Stockholm Olympic Stadium)

The stadium was built for the 1912 Olympic Games based on the plans of architect Torben Grut. To this day, major sports events continue to take place in what is now one of the oldest sports arenas still in regular use. The annual track & field meeting, which takes place in mid-June, is an intrinsic part of the Diamond League series. Since the stadium can only hold around 14,500 spectators, the atmosphere is almost homely. No other competitive arena has seen as many world records broken as here. The in the meantime listed stadium also provides the venue for music performances by international stars.

➕ 179 F3 ✉ Lidingövägen
🖥 www.stockholm.se/stadion
🕐 Mon–Fri 7am–9pm, Sat 7:30am–7pm, Sun 7:30am–9pm
🚇 Ropsten 💶 Free

Enjoying a break on Kungsholmen in Maelarpaviljongen restaurant in between sights

Where to...
Eat and Drink

Prices
for a main course without drinks
£ under kr200   ££ kr200–kr350   £££ over kr350

Berns Bar & Bistro ££–£££
Berns is cult and tradition rolled into one. The salons of this luxury 19th-century establishment were reconceived by the British designer Sir Terence Conran. From mussels to macaroons – this is where you can eat French food in style. Those who like it a little more exotic can go to Bern's Asiatiska. Berns can offer even more: good entertainment with music, either from a DJ or live.

🔲 181 F5 ✉ Berzelii Park
☎ 08 56 63 22 00; www.berns.se
🕐 Mon–Thu 11:30am–11pm,
Fri, Sat until midnight, Sun noon–10pm
🚇 Östermalmstorg, Kungsträdgården

Konditori Valand £

A visit to Valand is like a time journey back to 1954. Since it opened, this place has not changed a bit. From the fridge and chairs to the flooring, everything is original – no wonder that the café has been used as a film stage on numerous occasions, Only the cakes are naturally fresh and delicious.

🔲 178 C3 ✉ Surbrunnsgatan 48
☎ 08 30 04 76 🕐 Mon–Fri 9am–6pm,
Sat, Sun 11am–5pm 🚇 Rådmansgatan

Flippin Burgers £
This burger restaurant believes that good local meat and good organic bread produce a good-tasting burger – and that's what people want! It's also much more comfortable here than at that competitor chain.

🔲 178 C2 ✉ Observatoriegatan 8
ℹ www.flippinburgers.se
🕐 Mon–Fri 4pm–10pm, Sat, Sun noon–10pm
🚇 Odenplan

Grand Café Strömkajen £–££
The ultimate luxury hotel, the Grand Hôtel, is also a popular meeting place. In summer, it is a wonderful experience to sit outside on the quay under pastel-coloured parasols, watching the comings and goings of the skerry boats, as you eat your meal.

🔲 181 F4 ✉ Blasiholmen ☎ 08 6 79 35 00;
www.grandhotel.se 🕐 Summer daily 8am–6pm
🚇 Kungsträdgården 🚌 69 🚊 7

Il Caffe £
It would be easy to miss this tiny Italian café near Stadshuset. Stieg Larsson fans (*Millennium* Trilogy) might find it interesting though. The author regularly drank his cappuccino here.

🔲 180 B4 ✉ Bergsgatan 17 ☎ 08 6 52 30 04;
www.ilcaffe.se 🕐 Mon–Fri 8am–6pm, Sat, Sun
10am–6pm 🚇 Rådhuset

Kungshallen £
Stockholm's only restaurant complex with more than a dozen restaurants and low prices. Don't expect gourmet cuisine, rather a world trip from döner kebab via TexMex, Chinese and burger to pizza and pasta.

🔲 181 D5 ✉ Kungsgatan 44
ℹ www.kungshallen.eu
🕐 Basement: Mon–Sat 11–10, Sun noon–10,
Ground Floor: Mon–Sat 9am–11pm, Sat 11–11,
Sun noon–11pm 🚇 Högtorget

Operakällaren £££
Here people eat in festive surroundings. The cellar restaurant, which opened in the late 19th century, ranks with its historical murals and sculpted oak wood panels among

the most impressive restaurants in the town. Cuisine, wine menu and prices are oriented to the opera setting. Smaller, but still with a certain luxurious je ne sais quoi with its Art Nouveau interior, is the Café Opera, opened in 1905. The popular meeting place for artists, intellectuals and business people offers fine, international cuisine.

➕ 181 E4 ✉ Operahuset, Karl XII:s torg
☎ 08 6 76 58 00; www.operakallaren.se
🕐 Tue–Sat 6pm–10pm 🚇 Kungsträdgården

Petite France £

French through and through, from cakes and pastries to breakfast. Here you are served real croissants, pains au chocolat and brioches. It has adapted slightly to the Swedish way of life though, because you also get *kanelbulle* here. Brunch, at the weekend from 10am–3pm, is naturally with French specialities.

➕ 180 A4 ✉ John Ericssonsgatan 6
☎ 08 6 18 28 00; www.petitefrance.se
🕐 Mon–Fri 8am–6pm, Sat, Sun 9am–5pm
🚇 Rådhuset

Prinsen ££

Bistro and brasserie dating back to 1897 with a lot of charm and a classical interior. The popular meeting place of the intellectual scene offers a successful symbiosis of Swedish and French cuisine – fish soup and *köttbullar* amicably brought into each other's company on the menu. Descend the staircase to the Hemingway Bar; there you can listen to the music and try out the favourite cocktails of the hard-drinking writer.

➕ 181 F5 ✉ Mäster Samuelsgatan 4
☎ 08 6 11 13 31; http://restaurangprinsen.eu
🕐 Mon–Fri 11:30am–11pm, Sat 12:30pm–11:30pm, Sun 1pm–11:30pm
🚇 Östermalmstorg

Restaurang Jonas £££

From the outside, the HSB building presents an air of understatement. However, inside, nothing stands in the way of the culinary treats. There is a choice of daily menus only – the prices are reasonable and the menus change each day. They are always fresh and always surprising. The set menu is either for four or six courses, each with an appropriate wine. Those who order the All-in-Menu pay the princely sum of kr1,500 and almost the same again on top for the wine package.

➕ 180 B5 ✉ Flemminggatan 39
☎ 08 6 50 22 20; www.restaurangjonas.se
🕐 Tue–Sat 6pm–11pm
🚇 Fridhemsplan, Rådhuset

Stadshuskällaren ££–£££

For years, this noble restaurant in Stadshuset has been responsible for preparing the celebratory dinner as part of the Nobel Prize Award programme. The rest of the year anyone is allowed to book a table and let themselves be pampered by the prize-winning Andreas Hedlund. Renovated in 2012, the City Hall cellar now presents a successful mixture of modern design and historical setting. You can order the latest Nobel Prize Award menu, but it is better to order it a few days in advance. In principle, all of the menus since 1902 are also available, but only for groups of ten or more.

➕ 180 C4 ✉ Hantverkargatan 1
☎ 08 58 62 18 30; www.stadshuskallarensthlm.se
🕐 Mon, Tue 11:30am–2:30pm, Wed–Fri 11:30am–2:30pm, 5pm–11pm, Sat 5pm–11pm
🚇 T-Centralen 🚊 3

Vete-Katten £

A traditional café with a subtly modern atmosphere that is appealing. This is the right place for anyone staying in a hotel that does not serve breakfast. Or how about a piece of cake after wandering round the town, or would you prefer the afternoon tea buffet? The quality is beyond all doubt, guaranteed by pastry chef Johan Sandelin.

➕ 181 D5 ✉ Kungsgatan 55
☎ 08 20 84 05; www.vetekatten.se
🕐 Mon–Fri 7:30–7:30, Sat, Sun 9:30–6
🚇 Hötorget

Where to...
Shop

The most important shopping boulevard in Stockholm's centre, Drottninggatan, leads in a straight south to north line through Norrmalm. At the south end are the souvenir shops and bargain shops, around Sergels torg are the larger department stores and further north the more expensive boutiques. In Hamngatan there is one shop after another, and enthroned in the centre is the venerable Nordiska Kompaniet department store. Shopping is also good around Stureplan and in Birger Jarlsgatan.

DESIGN AND HANDICRAFTS

Swedish design is always a good choice because it has far more than just mass-produced products to offer. Clear forms, light colours, an eye for functionality, textiles with squares and stripes – those are the classics associated with Sweden. However, Swedish design is not limited to furniture and clothing; in the meantime it offers attractive solutions for almost every utensil used in everyday life. And it does not always have to be contemporary design. There are also many antique shops in Stockholm, a good area being – apart from Gamla Stan (▶ 75) – the Vasastan district.

Asplund (Sibyllegatan 31; www.asplund.org, metro: Östermalmstorg) sells the work of well-known designers. The furniture and carpets are generally in light colours and functional forms.

The selection from **Design Torget** (Sergelgången 29; tel: 08 4 62 35 20; www.designtorget.se, metro: T-Centralen) encompasses almost everything that one could

need in the home or that looks attractive. It is mainly young designers that present their work here. Other branches are in Kungsgatan, no. 52 (metro: Hötorget) and Nybrogatan no. 16 (metro: Östermalmstorg).

If you are looking for an accessory for the bathroom or kitchen or a souvenir, you will probably be lucky at **Iris Handverk** (Kungsgatan 55; tel: 08 39 90 90; www.irishantverk.se, metro: Hötorget). Tip: high-quality brushes made of natural materials, handmade.

Founded in 1913, the furniture store **Nordiska Galleriet** (Nybrogatan 11; tel: 08 4 42 83 60; www.nordiskagalleriet.se, metro: Östermalmstorg) offers modern classics by the best Scandinavian and international furniture designers.

Svenskt Tenn (Strandvägen 5; tel: 08 6 70 16 00; www.svenskt tenn.se, metro: Östermalmstorg) started in 1924 with design articles made of tin, hence the name. Yet its product range was soon extended to include every kind of household article. Many of the timeless and classic pieces are the legacy of the Austrian-Swedish architect and designer Josef Frank. Take the time to wander through the large shop on the refined Strandvägen and pop into the tea room where fine tea is available in a very pleasant setting.

DEPARTMENT STORES & SHOPPING ARCADES

Åhléns City (Klarabergsgatan 50; tel: 08 6 76 64 50; www.ahlens.com, metro: T-Centralen), Sweden's largest shopping chain with almost 100 shops has 17 branches in Greater Stockholm alone. The products give a good idea of Swedish interiors and of how you can furnish a place relatively inexpensively without having to go to Ikea.

The shopping arcade **Birger Jarlspassagen** (Birger Jarlsgatan 7–9, metro: Östermalmstorg) is over a hundred years old, and its display windows, lamps and wood-panelled walls make it look like a relic from another time. Even looking is experience enough – and, given the high prices, saves putting a hole in the holiday funds.

Moods (Regeringsgatan 48; tel: 08 4 11 87 11; www.mood stockholm.se, Bus: 69) is one of the latest luxury shopping centres in the centre with refined boutiques and diverse restaurants.

Every Stockholmer knows what the two letters mean: they are the hallmark of the traditional company **Nordiska Kompaniet** (Hamngatan 18; tel: 08 7 62 80 00; www.nk.se, metro: Kungsträdgården) and are written resplendently on its facade. Opened in 1902, the NK has always aimed to be on a par with London's Harrods and Berlin's KaDeWe.

Apart from the elegant products, the gourmet food hall is also worth closer attention. **Sturegallerian** (Stureplan 4; www.sturegallerian. se, metro: Östermalmstorg) is also a shopping arcade aimed at the fuller wallet. Around 60 shops with grand names keep good company under one roof.

SPORT & OUTDOORS

Outdoor fans really will find absolutely everything they need for a stay in the wilderness at the **Fjällräven Center** (Kungsgatan 26; tel: 08 54 51 86 88; www.fjallraven. se, metro: Hötorget). The Swedish company Fjällräven is one of the largest brands in the outdoor area.

BOOKS

Do you enjoy rummaging through old books? Then **Rönnells Antikvariat** (Birger Jarlsgatan 32; tel: 08 54 50 15 50; http://ronnells.se, metro: Östermalmstorg) is the ideal address. The largest second-hand bookshop in Stockholm has a fantastic choice of books in various languages. Readings take place in the evenings.

DELICATESSEN

Bondens egen marknad (Tessinparken, metro: Karlaplan, Bus: 1, 4) means "Farmers' Market" and takes place every Saturday from 10am–3pm in the summer. At you the market, you can buy fresh fruit and vegetables grown in the area around Stockholm, but also other foods, such as honey and jam – the majority of which are totally organic **Ejes Chokladfabrik** (Reik Dahlbergsgatan 25; tel: 08 6 64 27 09; www.ejeschoklad.se, metro: Karlaplan) serves more than 100 different chocolates and truffles which melt in your mouth and have chocoholics' hearts racing in no time – a perfect souvenir, in as far as the delicacies actually make it all the way home.

FASHION

Just to ensure that there are no misunderstandings: **Acne** (Norrmalmstorg 2; tel: 08 6 11 64 11; www.acnestudios.com, metro: Östermalmstorg) stands for "Ambition to Create Novel Expressions" or, in short, fashion for him and her. Even the shops themselves are design objects.

Anna Holtblad (Grev Turegatan 13; tel: 08 54 50 22 20; www.annaholt blad.se, metro: Östermalmstorg) is a young Swedish design for female fashion. Also **Filippa K** (Grev Turegatan 18; www.filippa-k.com, metro: Östermalmstorg), who also does men's fashions and has earned a reputation outside of Sweden as well.

Where to...
Go Out

Trendy Södermalm is not the only party address, Norrmalm and Östermalm provide night owls with plenty of options. Classical performances are available in the Opera (➤ 66), in the Konserthuset (➤ 57) and in the time-honoured Dramaten (➤ 64). The Kulturhuset (➤ 66) tends to focus on modern plays. The clubs offer Jazz, Rock and Pop, the nightlife centring around Stureplan. And last but not least, the cinemas are also a good option; almost all of the films are shown in the original version.

THEATRE & CONCERT VENUES

The Radio Symphony Orchestra and the Radio Choir play in **Berwaldhallen** (Oxenstiernsgatan 20; tel: 08 784 18 00; www. berwaldhallen.se, ticket sales Mon–Fri noon–6pm, Bus: 69, 76), a modern concert hall with excellent acoustics.

The **Chinateatern** (Berzelii Park 9; tel: 08 56 28 92 00; www.chinateatern.se, metro: Kungsträdgården) opened in 1928, Stockholm's largest private theatre, offers a broad programme of cabaret, musicals, revues and classical theatre.

Also offering a broad repertoire – from classical to experimental works: the **Stadsteatern** (Sergels torg 7; tel: 08 50 62 02 00; www. stadsteatern.stockholm.se, metro: T-Centralen).

Insider Tip During the summer, the ensemble of the Stadsteatern regularly goes on tour through the parks of the capital and performs under the name of **Parkteatern**. The free performances out in the open are popular and well attended.

ENTERTAINMENT

During carnival (Kungsgatan 63; tel: 08 53 48 29 60; www.fasching. se, metro: T-Centralen), the city's most well-known jazz club offers live music almost every night – which is not always jazz.

Nalen (Regeringsgatan 74; tel: 08 50 52 92 00; www.nalen.com, metro: Hötorget) is the home of Jazz, Rock and Pop; its restaurant mainly serves Swedish cuisine.

The **Oscarsteatern** (Kungsgatan 63; tel: 08 20 50 00; www.oscars teatern.se, metro: T-Centralen) is located in a wonderful 1906 theatre palace; however, no theatre plays are staged here any longer, just musicals.

A Stockholm institution and success story is **Wallmans Salonger** (Teatergatan 3; tel: 08 50 55 60 70; www.wallmans.se, metro: Kungsträdgården), which serves a good mix of high-class shows with dinner.

BARS, CLUBS & NIGHTLIFE

The **Café Opera** (Karl XII:s torg; tel: 08 6 76 58 07; www.cafeopera.se, metro: Kungsträdgården) is the city's most refined and well-known night club. This is where members of the prominent crowd meet.

Anyone who knows the cult series *Dallas* will be familiar with the name **Cliff Barnes** (Norrtullsgatan 45; tel: 08 31 80 70; www.cliff.se, metro: T-Centralen). While waiting in the queue in front of Cliff Barnes, you can think about what he has to do with his counterpart J. R. Ewing. Anyone who has managed to get in, eats the American food and waits until 11pm when the restaurant turns into a night club.

In the **Nordic C Hotel**, you *Insider Tip* can sit wrapped in a thermal coat in the ice bar (Vasaplan 4; tel: 08 50 56 30 00; http://nordicchotel. se/icebar; metro: T-Centralen) and sip a drink from ice glasses.

Gamla Stan

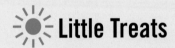 **Little Treats**

A Roof-Top View of Stockholm

During a tour of the **Roofs of Riddarholmen** (►87), you can view Stockholm's Old Town from a totally new perspective.

Evening Ramble

Those who can arrange to go for a walk through the **Old Town** (►79) after 6pm can experience the charm of the narrow streets without the jostling crowds.

Arrival by Boat

Take the **ferry** (►36) from Djurgården to Gamla Stan – the Old Town is best from the waterside.

Getting Your Bearings

The oldest part of Stockholm is also the most beautiful. In Gamla Stan, you have some of the most important sights in a very compact and manageable area.

A visit to the Royal Palace is a must on a tour through Gamla Stan. For some people just seeing the palace from the outside is enough, but most people visit at least the Royal Apartments and the Treasury. Those who arrive at midday can also take in the spectacle of the changing of the guard. In the immediate vicinity of the palace are the Storkyrkan, and Riddarholmen

Perfect Days in...

The restaurant Under Kastanjen is located on one of Stockholm's most beautiful squares, the small Brända tomten

A bird's eye view – here from the tower of Stadshuset – presents the panorama of Gamla Stan

Church, the city's most important places of worship. It is just a stone's throw to Stortorget Square, where you will find not only the Nobel Museum but also a whole row of cosy cafés and restaurants for a well-earned break. In the past, it was not as convivial on the square – Stortorget used to be Stockholm's place of execution.

The rest of the district continues on the other side of Västerlånggata, the high street of the Old Town. In the southern section of Gamla Stan, some particularly picturesque corners and squares await you. It is worth doing some exploring on your own, especially as there are far fewer tourists in this area. Most people stay in the palace area. You certainly can't get lost in Gamla Stan. This part of the town, located on an island, is so small that in either direction you reach the water after only a couple of hundred metres, so it is easy to get your bearings again.

The Perfect Day

You can visit the sights in Gamla Stan comfortably in one day. Those in a hurry need only half the time. Of course, you've then seen a lot but, in essence, only scratched at the surface. In Stockholm's Old Town there is so much to discover away from the main sights, which is why it is worth taking more time to wander around.

⏰ 10:00am

Strictly speaking the tour does not begin in Gamla Stan but on the tiny island of Riddarholmen, which is "attached" to the Old Town. Coming from the town centre, you reach Riddarholmen via Centralbron, from which you have a fantastic view of the **City Hall** (▶ 50). Past the **34** **Birger Jarls Tower** (▶ 94) you come to the ⭐ **Riddarholmen Church** (▶ 87), the burial church of the Swedish kings. It opens at 10am. It is worth taking the time to look inside; you can admire the tombs of 17 monarchs. Before you continue, take a quick look at the **Wrangel Palace** (▶ 88), which now houses the Svea Hovrätt, the Higher Regional Court.

⏰ 11:00am

Anyone wishing to visit the **29** **Riddarhuset** (House of Nobility, ▶ 91) needs to keep an eye on the time. The former assembly room of the Swedish aristocracy, in which, among other things, there are 2,331 coats of arms, is only open from 11am–noon.

⏱ 12:15

And it is also necessary to be on time for the next point on the programme.
The **Changing of the Guard at the palace** (➤ 84) takes place at 12:15pm –
a spectacle that you should not miss (an hour later on Sundays).

⏱ 1:00pm

Although you have the palace in front of you, it is worth – at least for those
who are hungry – making a stop at ★**Stortorget** (➤ 85; on the left). Don't
worry, it is only a few paces away. Sweden's most beautiful square is surrounded by many restaurants that offer a good lunch option. Afterwards,
you can then visit the **Nobel Museum** (➤ 86)

⏱ 2:30pm

The ★**Royal Palace** (➤ 80), naturally deserves a longer visit. Even for
a quick visit to the Representationsvåningarna (Royal Apartments)
and Skattkammaren (Treasury), you should plan at least one and a
half hours.

⏱ 4:00pm

The ㉘**Storkyrkan** (➤ 89), the Cathedral of Stockholm, is the church in
which the Swedish monarchy's coronations and marriages take place.
It adjoins the palace courtyard. (Please note: In the low season, the
church closes at 4pm)

⏱ 4:30pm

Now the tour continues along **Västerlånggata** (➤ 97). The pace may
be a little slower along this boulevard, because there is one shop after
the other, where you may
want to do some window-
shopping at the very
least.

⏱ 5:30pm

Wander through the
narrow little streets (on
the right) in the southern
part of Gamla Stan.
Don't miss a stop at the
picturesque, triangular
Brända tomten square.

⏱ 8:00pm

Stay in Gamla Stan,
where the stress of
day-to-day life seems
to evaporate and you
feel as though you have
travelled back in time.
A cosy meal option is
Under Kastanjen (➤ 97),
and elegance in the
star cuisine of **Frantzén**
(➤ 95).

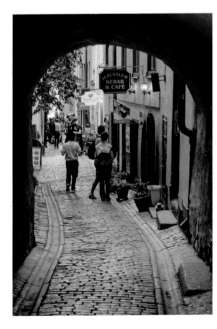

★ Kungliga Slottet
(Royal Palace)

The Kungliga slottet in Stockholm has over 600 rooms making it one of the largest palaces in Europe. It is where the king works and is still used for official receptions.

Built in the Baroque style, the Royal Palace was completed in 1750. It was not the first building on this site, however. Back in the 12th century, King Knut Eriksson had a small fortified castle built, about 100 years later a large fort followed. This, too, was continuously extended and converted. The result was the Tre Kronor (Three Crowns) castle, a potpourri of different building styles, which were regarded as relatively ugly.

That is why at the end of the 17th century it was decided to give the castle a new, more attractive appearance. However, plan after plan was ditched, so that the building work never really got going.

Baroque New Building

It must be seldom that a devastating fire is met with the enthusiasm with which the one in 1697 was met; it reduced the unpopular building to ashes and opened the way for the long-desired new start. **Nicodemus Tessin the Younger**, the greatest Swedish architect of the time was put in charge of building a new castle to replace the one that had burned down. At the time, Sweden was a great power, which is why it was legitimate to base the plans on the examples of another world power. The castle was conceived in the shape of a Roman palace. However, it soon became necessary to interrupt the ambitious project. In 1700, Sweden entered the Great Northern War against Saxony-Poland, Denmark and Russia, and the money for building the palace was needed in other areas. The Swedish king preferred to invest in weapons and cannons than in a palace, More and more workers were withdrawn from the then largest building site in Sweden. In 1709, building was stopped altogether.

The sound of hammers ceased for more than 15 years. It was not until 1726, five years after the end of the war, that building started again. Nicodemus Tessin was an old man in the meantime and did not live to see his masterpiece finished. He died in 1728. After him, **Carl Hårleman** continued the work based on his guidelines. It would be another 22 years until the palace was finally completed in 1750. Strictly speaking, it was not really ready then, since work carried on even after the building work was officially finished. And it took another 20 years until the interior work was complete.

Even now, work is being done on the palace – the exterior facade is being renovated. That is a Herculean task for such a huge building. The work is expected to be complete in 2036.

Since the palace is still being used by the Swedish royal family, it is only partially accessible. All the same: those who want to see everything can easily spend a whole day wandering through the palace on the trail of the Swedish kings.

Royal Apartments

The **Representationsvåningarna (State Rooms)** are the section of the Royal Apartments that are used when the king and queen receive guests at the palace. The original furnishing from the 17th century conveys an idea of the luxury that the royal family enjoyed at that time. You can, among other things, visit the bedroom of King Gustav III (with the bed in which the king died after he was attacked at the Royal Opera), Oscar II's writing room and the ornately furnished **Rikssalen (Hall of State)**. It was in the Hall of State that parliamentary meetings were held with the king to negotiate important matters. Today the room is used for banquets and concerts. The wedding celebration of Crown

The Royal Palace from Slottsbacken; in the background the rear facade of the Great Church

Gamla Stan

Princess Victoria and Daniel Westling took place here. Daniel Westling has since been given the title of Prince Daniel of Sweden, Duke of Västergötland.

Queen Christina's Silver Throne

The precious silver throne that now stands in the Hall of State was a present from Magnus Gabriel De la Gardie to Queen Christina on her coronation in 1650. De la Gardie was at that time one of the most important people in the country. His reasons for making such an expensive coronation present may not only have only been due to his reverence for Christina as his queen. Although it was never confirmed, there were strong rumours that De la Gardie was the queen's lover.

The throne was crafted in Augsburg in the south of Germany and was the only piece of furniture to survive the castle fire in 1697. Until well into the 1970s, the king took his place on the throne every year for the state opening of the Swedish parliament. In the meantime, however, the Swedes no longer want the king to play this prominent role, and since 1975 the delegates have opened the new session without a speech by the king. The two female statuettes on the left and right of the throne symbolise justice (holding a sword) and wisdom (holding a mirror).

The Treasury

The **Swedish Imperial Regalia** are exhibited in the Treasury. These include the crown, the sceptre, the orb and the key of King Erick XIV as well as the imperial sword of King Gustav Vasa, an Augsburg work from 1541. The last Swedish king, who was officially crowned, was Oscar II in 1873. Nonetheless, the imperial regalia was also used time and again, although without them being worn by the king or queen. When the King of Sweden, Carl Gustaf XVI married Queen Silvia in 1976, the crowns were placed on both sides of the altar.

Erik XIV's Imperial Key made of gilded silver can be viewed in the treasury

The Treasury holds plenty of other treasures for visitors to admire – royal crowns, splendid swords and jewels from many centuries.

Museums in the Palace

The **Tre Kronor** Museum presents the fascinating history of the castles that preceded the current palace. Gustav III's Museum of Antiquities (**Gustav III:s antikmuseum**) shows the sculptures and statues that the art-loving king collected during the course of his reign. Gustav III, who is best known in history for his murder at a masked ball in 1792, brought

A view of the opulently ornamented Baroque staircase of the Royal Palace

many exhibits back from his trip to Italy. Sometimes, however, His Majesty was not particularly adept when purchasing what he thought to be precious gems. Some of the pieces he purchased turned out to be fakes. The museum was opened in 1794 and is thus one of the oldest of its kind in Europe.

Swedish princes and princesses are traditionally baptised in the **Slottskyrkan (Royal Chapel)**. Every Sunday at 10am mass is held, and the service open to the public. During the summer, organ and classical concerts also take place in the chapel. Exhibited in the palace's **Livrustskammaren (Armoury)** are ceremonial props for parades, carriages, suits of armour, hunting weapons and the ceremonial costumes of Sweden's sovereigns.

The **Kungliga Myntkabinettet (Royal Coin Cabinet)**, which is directly opposite the entrance to the palace courtyard, has a very interesting exhibition about the history of the monetary system. You'd have to be very strong to pick up the heaviest coin in the world – it weighs 19.4kg (42.8lb), dates back to 1644 and is actually "only" a whopping copper plate. Sweden's oldest coins are much smaller and lighter. They are also on show in the Royal Coin Cabinet. They were introduced as a means of payment at the end of the 10th century by King Olof Skötkonung. People were a lot quicker in other countries – which is why visitors to the exhibition can see coins that are well over 2,000 years old but not of Swedish origin. It was actually the Chinese that introduced the first bank notes, probably just before the year 1000AD.

TAKING A BREAK

From mid-June to the third weekend in August a **café in Palace Courtyard** serves cakes, snacks and drinks.

Gamla Stan

➕ 181 E3–F4 ✉ Slottsbacken; www.kungahuset.se
🚇 13, 14, 17, 18, 19 Gamla Stan G2, 43, 55, 71, 76
💳 kr150 (applies for state rooms, treasury, Tre Kronor Museum and Gustav III's Museum of Antiquities)

State Rooms, Treasury and Tre Kronor Museum
☎ 08 4 02 61 30 (tours) mid-Sep–mid-May Tue–Sun 10am–4pm,
mid-May–end June daily 10am–5pm, July–Aug daily 10am–5pm,
state rooms from 8:30am, Aug–mid-Sep daily 10am–5pm
💳 see above

Gustav III's Museum of Antiquities
🕐 End of April–mid-May Tue–Sun 10am–4pm,
mid-May–mid-Sep daily 10am–5pm 💳 see above

Palace Chapel
🕐 Mid-May–mid-Sep 10am–5pm 💳 Free

Armoury
🕐 Sep–April Tue–Sun 11am–5pm, Thu until 8pm,
May–June daily 11am–5pm, July–Aug daily 10am–6pm
💳 Free

Royal Coin Cabinet
🕐 Daily 11am–5pm 💳 Free

INSIDER INFO

Insider Tip

No visit to the palace is complete without going to see 🏛 **The Changing of the Guard**. The ceremony is not quite as spectacular as in London, but the Swedish version is also a popular photo motif, which children will find fun too. It takes place every day at 12:15pm; on Sundays it is an hour later. On some days in summer, the **Life Guards Dragoons** take part in the Changing of the Guard. If you want to see the soldiers on horseback go online www.forsvarsmakten.se/sv/var-verksamhet/hogvakten/tid-och-plats-for-hogvakten.

⭐ Stortorget

Stortorget, the main square of Gamla Stan, is the oldest and probably most beautiful square in Stockholm. In the Middle Ages, it was a marketplace, too, but at that time also the site of the pillory.

In 1520 heads rolled on the Stortorget. That was when the king Christian II, subsequently "Christian the Tyrant" had almost 90 members of the Swedish aristocracy executed after they had planned an uprising against him. What was particularly perfidious about the whole episode was that the king had invited his opponents to Stockholm to celebrate with them at a reconciliation feast. People said that the whole square turned red from the blood of the beheaded men – which is why the day went down in history as the **"Stockholm Bloodbath"**. If it makes you feel any better: this cruel deed did not end well for the king. The murder caused an even larger uprising, resulting not only in Christian losing his crown in Sweden, but also in Denmark and Norway as well. Initially, Christian was able to escape to Holland, but when he tried to reconquer his throne, he was captured and imprisoned until his death in 1559.

The northern side of Stortorget is flanked by the stock market; in summer, this area is one of the most popular meeting places in town

German Legacy

All around the square are brightly coloured merchants' houses. None of them witnessed the Bloodbath of 1520, however, since the original buildings were all burnt to the ground during the Great Stockholm Fire of 1625. The houses that surround the square today date from the period after the fire. Many of them still have medieval vaulted cellars, which often provide the venue for a res- taurant. The German inscription in the entrance area of the **Grill House** (Grillska huset, Stortorget 3) also shows the great extent to which German immigrants influenced

the city during this period. Named after the goldsmith Anton Grill, who came to Stockholm from Augsburg in 1680, the building is now home to the café and bakery of the *Stadsmission* (City Mission).

Front of the Nobel Prize medal (magnified)

Nobelmuseet (Nobel Museum)

The former **Stock Exchange**, built by Erik Palmsted in 1778, now houses the Nobel Museum. Visitors can learn about the life of prize benefactor Alfred Nobel and the winners of the prestigious international award. The meetings of the Swedish Academy take place on the upper floor, and its 18 members decide on the winner of the Nobel Prize for Literature.

View of the exhibition in the Nobel Museum

TAKING A BREAK

There are a lot of cafés and restaurants around Stortorget. The **Nobel Museum Bistro** offers a special extra – and it is not of the culinary kind. Turn your chair upside down before you sit on it. You will find the signature of a Nobel Prize winner. The winners are asked to put their signature on the back of a chair when they visit the museum.

➕ 181 E3 🚇 13, 14, 17, 18, 19

Nobel Museum
✉ Stortorget 2
☎ 08 53 48 18 00;
www.nobelmuseum.se
🕐 Sep–May Tue 11am–8pm,
Wed–Sun 11am–5pm,
June–Aug daily 9am–8pm
💰 kr100 (Tue 5pm–8pm entry free)

INSIDER INFO

- Erik Palmstedt, the architect of the stock market also built his own home nearby. His address is no. **27 Västerlånggatan**.
- House no. 20 on **Stortorget** square deserves a closer look: the 82 white stones are apparently to commemorate the 82 aristocrats executed in 1520. Nobody really knows if the story is true or not, since the exact number of men killed on that day is not known
- From mid-November until 23 December is Stockholm's romantic and much loved **Christmas Market** (www.stortorgetsjulmarknad.com; daily 11am–6pm).

⭐9 Riddarholmskyrkan
(Riddarholmen Church)

The Riddarholmskyrkan is the burial church of the Swedish monarchs and also the only surviving medieval monastery church in Stockholm. It is named after the "Knights' Islet"– Riddarholmen – the little island to the west of the Old Town, now the centre of Stockholm's judiciary.

Riddarholmskyrkan, built at the end of the 13th century, was originally the church of a now no longer existing Franciscan monastery. Continually extended over the years, the church did not receive its eye-catching cast iron spire until 1841.

Interior

The **crypts and sarcophaguses of the 17 Swedish monarchs** are of particular interest. All of the monarchs that died between 1632 and 1950 are buried here; the only exception is Queen Christina, who abdicated in 1654 and converted to the Catholic faith. She is buried in Rome. There are also some tombs of Swedish monarchs from the Middle Ages, including those of Magnus Ladulås and Karl Knutson Bonde.

The eye-catching brick tower of Riddarholmen Church is visible for miles

Gamla Stan

The two **Baroque** burial chapels of Karl X and Gustav II Adolf on the left and right of the altar are particularly impressive. Also very worth seeing are the numerous **coat of arms of the Order of the Seraphim** adorning the walls of the church. Until 1820, the deceased knights of this Order were buried here. During funeral processions from the palace to the church, the coat of arms of the respective knight accompanied the coffin, and after the coffin had been interred the coat of arms was hung on the church wall.

Wrangelska palatset

Wrangelska palatset (Wrangel Palace, Birger Jarls torg no. 16) is in the immediate vicinity of Riddarholmskyrkan. The palace has housed Svea hovrätt (Svea Court of Appeal) since 1756. The oldest sections of the palace date back to the 1530s; its current appearance is the result of extensions and conversions done between 1652 and 1670 Queen Kristina had bought the palace shortly beforehand. After the building work had been completed, she gave it to field marshal Carl Gustav Wrangel in reward for his services as a military commander during the Thirty Years' War (i. a. Wrangel was governor-general of Swedish Pomerania). Wrangel Palace was the biggest private palace in the city and thus served as the king's residence after the Stockholm Great Fire between the years of 1697 and 1754.

For a short time Wrangel Palace served as the royal residence

TAKING A BREAK

Insider Tip In the restaurant aboard the refurbished yacht **Mälardrottningen** (➤ 41) non-hotel guests can also enjoy a meal or a coffee. In the summer, you can eat al fresco on the deck.

➕ 181 E3 ✉ Birger Jarls Tower

Riddarholmen Church
🕐 May–mid-Sep daily 10am–5pm, mid-Sep–Nov Sat, Sun 10am–4pm
🚋 13, 14, 17, 18, 19 🎫 kr50 (only with ticket, cash payment at the ticket office of the Royal Palace and online purchase possible)

INSIDER INFO

Insider Tip Join a **roof-top tour** and enjoy a bird's eye view of Riddarholmen and Gamla Stan – the shot of adrenaline it gives you is free of charge. For details, see www.takvandring.com/en/home, kr595.

28 Storkyrkan
(The Great Church)

Located directly next to the Royal Palace, at the top of Slottsbacken (street), is Storkyrkan, the capital's cathedral dedicated to St Nicholas and also known as Sankt Nikolai.

Time and again, the maze of alleys in the Old Town reveal a view of Storkyrkan

Stokyrkan is one of the oldest churches in the town, although nobody knows exactly when it was built. The town founder Birger Jarl is thought to have commissioned its construction in the mid-13th century. It is first mentioned in a written source in 1279 when a knight sentenced to death bequeathed all his possessions to the church. By 1480, comprehensive renovation work extended the church to its current size. The facade, as it is today, was reconstructed from 1736 to 1742 to match the Royal Palace. In the 66m (217ft) high **church tower** of Storkyrkan hang four church bells, the largest of which weighs 4.5t.

The Cathedral Interior

The ebony **altar** dates back to the 17th century; its central panel was made in Germany, the wings in Stockholm. Also German craftsmanship is the 15th century 3.70m (12ft) tall, seven-armed **candelabrum** in front of the altar. Hanging in the northern side aisle is a painting by David Klöcker Ehrenstrahl (►92) from 1696, depicting the Last Judgment. In the central nave are two magnificent **royal chairs**. They were designed by Nicodemus Tessin the Younger in 1684. (Among other things, Tessin also built the Royal Palace.) Till this day, only members of the royal family are allowed to sit on these chairs.

Behind the French Baroque **pulpit** from around 1700 is the tomb slab of the Swedish reformer Olaus Petri. In the southern nave aisle hangs the **Vädersolstavla (Sun Dogs)**; the painting shows a mock sun apparition from 1535 and is the first known depiction of Stockholm. The original picture has been lost. In the church hangs a copy from around 1630.

The church's greatest treasure is the oak sculpture of **St George and the Dragon**, carved by the Lübeck sculptor Bernt Notke and inaugurated in 1489. It was commissioned by the Swedish regent Sten Sture the Elder. The figure of the dragon killers is supposed to symbolize Sten Sture, the dragon the Danish king, and the princess the rescued city of Stockholm. In front of the church is a 1898 statue of reformer Olaus Petri.

Coronation and Wedding Church

Storkyrkan used to be the coronation church of the Swedish monarchs, the last ceremony to take place there being in 1873 when Oscar II was crowned. His successor Gustav V discontinued this tradition on the occasion of his own investiture in 1907. The members of the Swedish royal family still marry in the church: in June 1976 Carl XVI Gustav and Queen Silvia, and in 2010 their daughter Crown Princess Victoria and Daniel Westling. And in May 2012, Crown Princess Estelle was baptised here.

The five-nave church has maintained its Brick Gothic interior; the exterior was later reconstructed in the Baroque style

TAKING A BREAK

The **Kaffegillet** restaurant (➤ 96) is only a few paces away from Storkyrkan and the Royal Palace. It offers hearty traditional meals.

➕ 181 E3
✉ Slottsbacken
☎ 08 7 23 30 00
🕐 Sep–May daily 9am–4pm, June also Mon–Fri until 5pm, July, Aug until 6pm
🚋 13, 14, 17, 18, 19 Gamla Stan
💰 kr40 (in autumn and winter for a donation)

INSIDER INFO

Guided tours are offered through the cathedral (kr40/pers.). You book them in advance by mail: info@stockholmsdomkyrkoforsamling.se.

㉙ Riddarhuset
(House of Nobility)

The Riddarhuset is regarded as one of Sweden's most beautiful palaces. In the Great Hall on the first floor is a unique collection of 2,331 coats of arms of the Swedish nobility.

The neoclassical House of Nobility was built between 1641 and 1674. Over the more than 30 years of construction, several architects were put in charge of the planning. The Dutchman Justus Vingboons was largely in charge of the exterior facade and took his inspiration for the design from the traditional construction style in his homeland. The two wings on the left and right of the building were added in 1870.

As the name indicates, the House of Nobility was commissioned by the Swedish nobility who held assemblies

Gustav Vasa, King of Sweden, receives visitors at the House of Nobility

here. Naturally the location of the building, within sight of the palace, was not coincidental – it was intended to indicate power.

A FINE FAMILY

A tragic story surrounds the architect who was first commissioned with the building. The Frenchman Simon de la Vallée was beaten to death by the city drunk a year after construction started. Since the murderer, Colonel Erik Oxenstierna, was related to Lord High Chancellor Axel Oxenstierna, he got away with just a small fine. A statue of the Lord High Chancellor stands on the north side of the building.

Gamla Stan

The Great Hall

A monumental staircase leads to the building's main sight, The Great Hall, on the first floor. Although the **copper shields** are the highlight, don't forget to look up at the ceiling. The ceiling fresco from the 1670s is the work of David Klöcker Ehrenstrahl, the then most renowned painter in the country. The allegorical painting *Dygdernas rådslag (The Crown of Immortality)* shows Mother Svea on the throne; hovering above her are three Graces holding crowns in their hands. It is intended to give the observer the feeling that the ceiling of the Riddarhuset opens up to heaven. Indirectly, the work contributed to Ehrenstrahl's coat of arms hanging in the Great Hall. David Klöcker, born in Hamburg in 1629, did not move to Stockholm until 1652. Thanks to his artistic skills, he soon advanced to be the favourite of the Swedish queen, Hedwig Eleonora of Holstein-Gottorp. The royal family was so enamoured with the painting in the House of Nobility that Klöcker was made a knight and permitted to add "Ehrenstrahl" to his name.

The many coats of arms cover practically all of the wall space in the Great Hall

Sculptural Decoration

Adorning the roof are several statues, the originals of which were built in the time around 1660. Today, what you see are all copies; the allegorical statues depict the **virtues** that a knight should have. The statue in front of the main entrance, cast in 1773, shows **Gustav Vasa**, the King of Sweden. It is believed to be the first memorial ever to appear on a public square in Sweden. The metal for its production was obtained from the old cannons that Karl XII had plundered from his enemies during his many battles. It was on this square in front of the Riddarhuset that the murderer of Gustav III was beheaded.

TAKING A BREAK

De Peppe (Storkyrkobrinken 16), a nice Italian restaurant within sight of Riddarhuset, which serves, among other things, decent pizzas.

➕ 181 E3 ✉ Riddarhustorget 10 ☎ 08 7 23 39 90; www.riddarhuset.se
🕐 Daily 11am–noon 🚋 13, 14, 17, 18, 19 Gamla Stan 💶 kr60

INSIDER INFO

Insider Tip

The painter David Klöcker Ehrenstrahl left a **tip** as to how best to appreciate his painting, *The Last Judgment*. You should stand directly beneath it, not in the middle, rather so that you are a bit closer to the eastern side (this is the left side when you are facing towards the palace). Give it a try!

At Your Leisure

30 Finska kyrkan (Finnish Church)

Opposite the palace is the simple church of the Finnish community. Originally erected as an indoor tennis court, the building was converted into a church in 1725. Stockholm's smallest sculpture crouches behind the church in the small park. Make a wish and stroke the head of the 14cm (5.5in) **Järnpojke**, iron boy, three times and your wish will be fulfilled in the same year. There are

Insider Tip

generally a few coins at the figure's feet. That is because the boy rewards anyone who gives him money with great wealth. To ensure that the Järnpojke does not catch cold in the winter, the Stockholmers wrap him up in a hat and scarf.

✚ 181 F3 ✉ Slottsbacken 2B–C
☎ 08 4 40 82 00
🚊 13, 14, 17, 18, 19 Gamla Stan

31 Tyska Kyrkan (German Church)

Many Germans have lived in Stockholm since the Hanseatic period. The St Gertrude Parish is thus the oldest German-speaking foreign community.

The church was built in the 14th century. Its present appearance was the result of conversion

Gamla Stan's landmark: the church tower of Tyska kyrkan

work in the 16th and 17th centuries. The **tower** was added in 1879 after its predecessor was destroyed by a fire. It was built by the Berlin architect Julyus Carl Raschdorff, the architect of the Berlin Cathedral. At 96m (315ft), the tower of the German Church is the highest point in the Old Town. Its **historical organ**, which dates back to 1608, is very interesting. The carillon is heard over the town at 8am and 4pm and is the prelude for two well-known hymns: *Praise the Lord* and *Now Thank We All Our God*.

✚ 181 E3 ✉ Svartmangatan 16
☎ 08 4 11 11 88; www.svenskakyrkan.se
🕐 May–mid-June daily 11am–3pm, mid-June until mid-Aug daily 10:30am–4:30pm, mid-Aug–mid-Sep daily 11am–3pm, mid-Sep until April Wed, Fri, Sat 11am–3pm, Sun 12:30pm–3pm
🚊 13, 14, 17, 18, 19 Gamla Stan

32 Riksdagshuset (Parliament House)

Presiding opposite the palace on the islet of Helgeandsholmen is the Swedish parliament. The **first building** was erected between 1896 and 1906 in the neoclassical style with a Baroque Revival facade section.

Gamla Stan

King Gustav Vasa and King Gustav Adolf are honoured with two portraits. The semi-circular new building, in which the parliament sessions take place was built in the 1970s.

➕ 181 E4 ✉ Riksgatan3A ☎ 08 7 86 40 00; www.riksdagen.se/en/visit-the-riksdag
🕐 Tours in English mid-Sep–June Sat, Sun, in the calendar weeks 26–34 also Mon–Fri, exact times on the internet 🚌 10, 11 Kungsträdgården

33 Bondeska palatset (Bonde Palace)

If you go from Norrmalm via Vasabron to the Old Town island of Stadsholmen, the first thing you will see on the left is the Bonde palace, an H-shaped, representative building with a small **Baroque garden**. It was built based on the plans of Nicodemus Tessin the Elder and Jean de la Vallée for the Bonde family from 1662–1673. The palace received its present shape after its reconstruction following a fire in 1753. As the family was increasingly plagued by financial problems, it had to eventually sell the building.

Since then, it has accommodated a number of different institutions, including The Royal Library and the City Hall. Since being extensively renovated in the 1940s, the building has served as the base of the Swedish Supreme Court.

➕ 181 E3 ✉ Riddarhustorget 8
🕐 not open to the public
🚌 13, 14, 17, 18, 19 Gamla Stan

34 Birger Jarls torn (Birger Jarl's Tower)

Constructed at the beginning of the 16th century to defend the town, the white tower on the north-western tip of Riddarholmen Island now nestles among the taller buildings that appeared over the following centuries. King Gustav Vasa is believed to have initiated the project. He allowed stones from The Convent of St Clare on Norrmalm, destroyed during the Reformation, to be used for the tower. The tower, which initially only had two storeys, underwent various conversions – also involving the adjoining buildings – during the course of which it received another two storeys. A 17th-century legend claims that the reason it is named after the city founder is because it is exactly at this spot that Birger Jarl founded Stockholm. Regardless of whether this story is true or not, there is a good view of Stadshuset from the foot of the tower.

➕ 181 D3 ✉ Norra Riddarholmshamnen
🕐 not accessible to the public 🚌 13, 14, 17, 18, 19 Gamla Stan

Sweden's centre of power: the parliament buildings

Where to...
Eat and Drink

Prices
for a main course without drinks
£ under kr200   ££ kr200–kr350   £££ over kr350

Gamla Stan is a small town district with a huge choice of restaurants. However, since there are a lot of city visitors in this area, there are unfortunately a lot of tourist traps as well, which serve bad and overly priced meals. At the same time, some of the city's best and most renowned restaurants are also located here. Owing to the special atmosphere of the Old Town, you should come here for dinner at least once.

Cultur ££

This cosy wine and tapas bar in the south of Gamla Stan is popular with the locals for its small after-work snacks, especially on Wednesdays when "Cava after work" is served between 5pm and 8pm. The glass of sparkling wine then only costs kr40 – which is a mega bargain for Swedish standards.

🚩 181 F3 ✉ Österlånggatan 34
☎ 08 22 66 66; www.culturbar.se
🕐 Tue–Thu 5pm–11pm, Fri, Sat 4pm–midnight
🚇 13, 14, 17, 18, 19 Gamla Stan
⛴ Djurgårdsfärjan

Djuret £££

Not for vegetarians and yet perfect for all those who like to be eco-logically responsible about what they eat. In Djuret, which means "animal", the name says it all. There is a vegetarian menu, but meat is celebrated here, so those who only eat vegetables and salad will probably not feel completely happy here. The meat prepared here is from animals reared according to the highest standards, and the first-class quality of the meat speaks for itself. The vegetables and salad also come from organic farms. As a guest, you have to rely on the chef's selection – the only choice you have is whether you order from the menu for the large or small appetite (Stora Djuret/Lilla Djuret kr755/kr595). There is a good reason for the "limited" choice. Only one animal is killed and prepared each time. The wine menu is in a class of its own and the home-brewed beer is also excellent. The furnishing is cosy-rustic in style and picks up "animal" and "hunting" themes.

🚩 181 E3 ✉ Lilla Nygatan 5
☎ 08 50 64 00 84; www.djuret.se
🕐 Mon–Sun 5:30pm–11pm,
Fri for lunch from noon
🚇 13, 14, 17, 18, 19 Gamla Stan

Fem Små Hus £££

Top cuisine in the heart of Gamla Stan. In its historic cellar rooms, the guests are entertained to Nordic cuisine with a French flair. The name of the restaurant "Five Little Houses" is based on the fact that the cellar stretches under five houses.

🚩 181 F3 ✉ Nygränd 10
☎ 08 10 87 75; http://femsmahus.se
🕐 Mon, Tue 5pm–11pm, Thu–Sat 5pm–midnight
🚇 13, 14, 17, 18, 19 Gamla Stan

Frantzén £££

The two star cooks Björn Frantzén and Daniel Lindberg are awarded stars by Guide Michelin year after year – this time they received two stars. Frantzén also regularly appears on the list of the 50 best restaurants worldwide. There is no menu. What is served up at the table depends on which top quality ingredients were available. The chefs dedicate their skills to Nordic cuisine, but are not averse to adding a touch of Asian refinement. Despite being such a high-class act, the restaurant's atmosphere is refreshingly unpretentious. Definitely reserve in advance – at least two weeks in advance.

🔶 181 E3 ✉ Lilla Nygatan 21
☎ 08 20 85 80; www.restaurantfrantzen.com
🕓 Tue–Thu from 6:30pm, Fri from 5pm, Sat from 3pm
🚊 13, 14, 17, 18, 19 Gamla Stan

The Flying Elk £££

Perhaps you don't wish to pay for the star-quality cuisine at Frantzén or you didn't get a table? Yet you still want to eat in a restaurant run by the star chef. Then The Flying Elk is the right choice. Nordic cuisine of the finest quality, at the weekend for lunch even hamburgers and cheeseburgers.

🔶 181 E3 ✉ Mälartorget 15
☎ 08 20 85 83; www.theflyingelk.se
🕓 Mon–Thu 5pm–midnight, Fri 5pm–1am, Sat noon–1am, Sun noon–midnight
🚊 13, 14, 17, 18, 19 Gamla Stan

Den Gyldene Freden £££

The classic choice in Gamla Stan. Guests have been served here since 1722. That makes "The Golden Peace" the oldest restaurant in the world. The well-known Swedish singer and popular poet Carl Michael Bellmann (1740–1795) not only used to eat and drink regularly in the restaurant, it is also immortalised in many of his songs. Nowadays, the restaurant serves typical Nordic dishes in a modern style. Main dishes start at about kr300, the prices are lower during the week at lunchtime and between 5pm and 6pm.

Insider Tip

🔶 181 F3 ✉ Österlånggatan 51
☎ 08 24 97 60; http://gyldenefreden.se
🕓 Mon–Fri 11:30am–10pm, Sat 1pm–10pm
🚊 13, 14, 17, 18, 19 Gamla Stan

Kaffegillet ££

The restaurant is located in a 14th-century cellar near the palace. It is a favourite tourist restaurant. Nonetheless, the owners have resisted the temptation to just focus on making easy money. The sound traditional fare does not need to shun comparison.

🔶 181 E3 ✉ Trångsund 4 ☎ 08 21 39 95
🚊 13, 14, 17, 18, 19 Gamla Stan

Kornhamstorg No. 53 £

This restaurant, reopened in December 2014, bears a name that is also its address. There is nothing exceptional about the menu, but the pizza and burgers are very satisfactory. There is brunch on Sundays. At the tables behind the large window, you have a box seat and can watch the comings and goings on the square in front of you.

🔶 181 E3 ✉ Kornhamstorg 53
☎ 08 20 90 33; www.no53.se
🕓 Mon–Tue 11am–11pm, Wed, Thu 11am–midnight, Fri 11am–1am, Sat noon–1am, Sun noon–11pm
🚊 13, 14, 17, 18, 19 Gamla Stan, Slussen

Le Rouge ££–£££

The name of the French brasserie is supposed to remind you of the Moulin Rouge in Paris. Guests sit under heavy canopies and it feels a bit like being in a tent. The restaurant specialises in two dishes, salmon and entrecote

🔶 181 F3 ✉ Brunnsgränd 2–4
☎ 08 51 80 40 00; www.lerouge.se
🕓 Tue 5pm–11pm, Wed, Thu until midnight, Fri, Sat until 1am
🚊 13, 14, 17, 18, 19 Gamla Stan

Tweed ££

If you only want to eat something light and focus the evening's intake on drinks, then the Tweed, which is in the same building as Djuret (➤ 95) is a good choice. You sit comfortably in the deep armchairs and can enjoy beers from small breweries.

⊞ 181 E3
✉ Lilla Nygatan 5
☎ 08 50 64 00 82; www.tweedbar.se
◑ Mon–Thu 5pm–midnight,
Fri 3pm–1am, Sat 5pm–1am
◎ 13, 14, 17, 18, 19 Gamla Stan

Under Kastanjen £

On the homepage, the restaurant boasts to be on Stockholm's most beautiful square. It is an opinion that one can share – the small Brända tomten is a feast for the eyes (ill. ► 76). Thus, it is worth going there for the location alone. What is more, the food, delicious traditional fare, makes the visit doubly worthwhile. The excellent bread come from the restaurant's own bakery. Inexpensive lunch menus from 11am–4pm.

Insider Tip

⊞ 181 F3 ✉ Kindstugatan 1
☎ 08 21 50 04; www.underkastanjen.se
◑ Mon–Fri 8am–11pm,
Sat 9am–11pm, Sun 9am–9pm
◎ 13, 14, 17, 18, 19 Gamla Stan, Slussen

Where to...
Shop

As far as shopping is concerned, Gamla Stan covers the entire spectrum. To start with, there is an endless range of souvenir shops, which at times offer bad quality and are rightly referred to as "tourist traps". But there are some real pearls as well: antique shops, galleries, shops with high-class Nordic design and boutiques that sell souvenirs – but quality pieces. The two main shopping boulevards that define Gamla Stan are the Västerlånggata on the one side of the island and Österlånggata on the other.

Many people associate Sweden with the Vikings. If you want to buy a Viking souvenir that is not a plastic helmet or wooden sword, then go to **Handfaste** (Västerlånggatan 73; www.handfaste.se, metro: Gamla Stan). There you will find all sorts of gifts to do with these strong men of the north which have a real historical reference.

At **E. Torndahl** (Västerlånggatan 63; www.etorndahl.se/en, metro: Gamla Stan) even the name of the shop inspires confidence – no forced play on words, just the name of the owner. Ida Thekla Sabina Kunigunda Thorndahl founded the shop in 1864, it has been run by the family ever since. It used to sell jewellery, now its sells the finest in Scandinavian design. The choice of products ranges from sunglasses, writing pads and soap to coffee cups, kitchen utensils and children's toys – what they all have in common is quality. Equally worth mention is the extremely friendly service.

Hilda Hilda (Österlånggatan 21, metro: Gamla Stan, open until 4pm) is a very special shop – because everything here is crafted by hand and "made in Sweden". The main focus is on accessories that can be used in the bathroom and the kitchen, i.a. tablecloths, cushion covers, tea towels, coasters, bags, bathroom towels and toiletry bags. It is worth going to Hilda Hilda.

You can find some really quirky children's toys in the small shop 🎎 **Kalikå** (Österlånggatan 18; www.kalika.se, closed on Sun, Mon). Some of the things are so original that a tour round the shelves is even fun for adults without children.

Insider Tip

Blå Gungan (Österlånggatan 16; www.blagungan.se/sv, metro: Gamla Stan) is a design shop with everything you need and a lot that you don't really need (but is fun all the same) for your home. You can even buy jewellery.

Gamla Stan's 🎎 **Polkagriskokeri** (Lilla Nygatan 10; www.gamlastans polkagriskokeri.se, metro: Gamla

Stan) sells *polkagrisar* (typical Swedish sticks of rock). They are traditionally red and white and taste of peppermint. In the meantime, they are available in every imaginable colour and flavour combination. This treat was made for the first time at the end of the 19th century – in the town of Gränna. These sticks of rock have been favourites with those of a sweet tooth all over Sweden. In Gamla Stan's Polkagriskokeri, you can not only choose between an endless number of varieties, you can also watch how *polkagrisar* is made and, if you book in advance, even learn how to make it yourself.

Where to...
Go Out

Gamla Stan tends to be the hunting ground of the older crowd. The people you meet are more interested in a good glass of wine in a relaxed ambience than clubbing to the small hours. Although some live venues can be found, they, too, are more likely to be acoustic guitar than electro beat. Otherwise, there are a few gay bars in Gamla Stan.

Corner Club
In the same street and under the same management as the starred restaurant Frantzén (➤ 95), the Corner Club offers a good atmosphere for the cocktail after the meal. The men (and the one woman) at the bar are not only masters of their profession but can tell you quite a bit about the drinks they are mixing.
➕ 181 E3 ✉ Lilla Nygatan 16
☎ 08 20 85 83; www.cornerclub.se
🕐 Tue 5pm–midnight, Wed–Sat 5pm–1am
🚃 13, 14, 17, 18, 19 Gamla Stan

Engelen
Bar, steakhouse and nightclub with live events – all under one roof. In this former chemist's, the only prescriptions filled are to cure hunger and thirst. The minimum age is 23.
➕ 181 E3 ✉ Kornhamnstorg 59B
☎ 08 20 10 92; www.engelen.se
🕐 Restaurant daily 5pm–midnight, Pub Mon–Thu 4pm–1am, Fri 4pm–3am, Sat noon–3am, nightclub Wed–Sat 10pm–3am
🚃 13, 14, 17, 18, 19 Gamla Stan 💃 Nightclub kr80–kr120, free for restaurant guests

The Secret Garden
During the day, The Secret Garden is a restaurant that serves small dishes; in the evening, it turns into a (wine) bar or nightclub. Perfect location with super view. On Wednesday evenings, there is a DJ and the dance floor is mainly populated by the gay crowd.
➕ 181 E3 ✉ Kornhamnstorg 59
☎ 08 59 90 19 59; www.secretgardensthlm.se
🕐 Daily noon–3am
🚃 13, 14, 17, 18, 19 Gamla Stan, Slussen

Torget
Opened in 2000, the Torget is one of Stockholm's oldest gay bars. The little restaurant serves good food, but the focus is mainly on drinks. There is a DJ on Fridays – and the bar generally gets very full.
➕ 181 E3 ✉ Mälartorget 13 ☎ 08 20 55 60; www.torgetbaren.com 🕐 Daily 5pm–1am
🚃 13, 14, 17, 18, 19 Gamla Stan

Pharmarium
In the place where Sweden's oldest pharmacy (1575) used to give out medicine, cocktails are now handed across the bar. To enable guests to line their stomach, small dishes can be ordered with the drinks they create themselves. In 2015 Pharmarium was elected the best bar of Stockholm by the respected daily *Dagens Nyheter*.
➕ 181 E3 ✉ Stortorget 7 ☎ 08 20 08 10; http://pharmarium.se 🕐 Sun–Tue 4:30pm–11pm, Wed, Thu until midnight, Fri, Sat until 1am
🚃 13, 14, 17, 18, 19 Gamla Stan, Slussen

Djurgården, Skeppsholmen & Kastellholmen

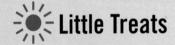 **Little Treats**

Totally Organic
In the greenhouse café of **Rosendals Trädgård** (► 130), you can enjoy a cup of coffee and homemade cake.

Gently Gliding Along
The **Sjöcaféet** (► 130) by the Djurgården Bridge rents out canoes and kayaks. Relaxing in one of these, you can experience Stockholm from the water.

Watching the Boats
Seek a sunny place in **Waldemarsudde** Park (► 115) and watch the to-ing and fro-ing of the boats.

Djurgården, Skeppsholmen & Kastellholmen

Getting Your Bearings

Djurgården Island, once the royal zoo, is now the green lung of the city. This is where the Stockholmers relax and have fun as well as indulge their love of art. The much smaller islands of Skeppsholmen and Kastellholmen are also calm oases in the middle of the city and offer a number of interesting museums.

As soon as you cross the Djurgården Bridge, you are spoilt for choice as to which museum you bestow your favour on first. The proud warship *Vasa* which sank on its maiden voyage and the Skansen Open-Air Museum should be right up at the top of your list. ABBA fans will no doubt want to go and see Agnetha, Björn, Benny and Anni-Frid, art friends will find the Waldemarsudde or Thiel Gallery more appealing.

Top 10

★ Vasamuseet (Vasa Museum) ➤ 104
★ Skansen ➤ 109
★ ABBA The Museum ➤ 112
★ Waldemarsudde ➤ 115

Don't Miss

For ABBA fans, an absolute must on Djurgården: ABBA The Museum

Afterwards for a little relaxation, you might want to visit the pleasure park Gröna Lund. Or perhaps take a walk by the water where you can watch the many boats arriving and leaving the harbour. Awaiting you on Skeppsholmen is the next cultural highlight: the Moderna museet. And even here relaxation is not in short supply – just wander over to Kastellholmen and enjoy the view across to the Old Town Gamla Stan!

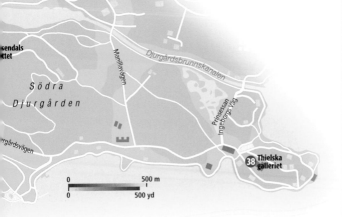

At Your Leisure

The Perfect Day

You need at least a whole day for the most important sights of Djurgården, Skeppsholmen and Kastellholmen. With so many museums, you will have to make a shortlist. On this tour, you will see the most important sights.

🕘 09:00am

Begin the day with a pleasant walk from the National Museum over Skeppsholmen Bridge. Take a look at the three-master *af Chapman* (➤ 127), and then wander further on to the small island of ⑩ **Kastellholmen** (➤ 126) and enjoy the panoramic view across the water. Then it is time to move on to the Museum of Modern Art that opens at 10am; before you go in, you should have time to view the fantasy figures in front of the museum.

🕙 10:00am

An impressive collection of works by Swedish and North European artists awaits you inside the ㊟ **Museum of Modern Art** (➤ 117). It includes international greats such as Picasso, Dalí, Oppenheim and Penn. After so much wonderful art, you should allow yourself a little break in the museum restaurant and enjoy one of the best views of Stockholm.

🕚 11:30am

The **Djurgårdsfärjan** (➤ 36) brings you to Djurgården in just a few minutes. After a short walk, you arrive at the entrance of the ⭐ **Skansen Open-Air Museum** (➤ 109; top), for which you need to be fairly mobile. The around 150 historical buildings are spread over 30ha (74 acres)! Do you want one of the typical Swedish *köttbullar*? Then the **Skansen Terrassen** restaurant (➤ 111) is exactly right for you. Equally typical is the *smörgåsbord* (Swedish Buffet) in the **Sollidens Restaurang** (➤ 111).

⏰ 1:30pm

Just a few minutes away, the next museum highlight awaits you: ☆**Vasa Museum** (➤ 104). In the dim hall, the dark oak hull of the boat with its many embellishments looks particularly impressive.

⏰ 3:30pm

Get into a tram at the Vasa Museum and stay in it until the last stop. After a short walk, you reach the ☆**Waldemarsudde** (➤ 115), where you can view the artworks of the painter prince Eugen in his former beautifully situated villa. Those who are more interested in contemporary musical masterpieces may prefer to see what the Swedish pop icons have to offer at ☆**ABBA The Museum** (➤ 112).

⏰ 6:00pm

After the tiring museum tour, how about something light-hearted to finish the day's programme? Sweden's oldest amusement park **41 Gröna Lund** (➤ 127) offers attractions that include the big dipper and many other funfair rides, as well as concerts and numerous restaurants.

⏰ 8:00pm

Those who don't stop for food in Gröna Lund should do so in **Wärdshuset Ulla Winbladh** (➤ 130); the restaurant serves refined traditional Swedish cuisine.

⭐2 Vasamuseet
(Vasa Museum)

The *Vasa* was the prestige project of King Gustav II Adolf. With its size and firing power, he wanted to impress friend and foe alike, as well as establish Sweden as a major world power. However, the pride of the Swedish fleet sank on her maiden voyage in 1628. It took another 333 years before the wreck could be salvaged. It is now on show in a museum built specially for it: The 🏛 Vasa Museum is one of Stockholm's largest tourist magnets.

10 August 1628: It was a beautiful sunny day with a light breeze – a perfect day to launch the new battleship *Vasa*. Many Stockholmers had come to be present at the extravaganza and celebrate in style. Captain Söfring Hansen ordered the sails to be hoisted and there was a gun salute. Yet after just a few metres the ship heeled dangerously, and the first stronger gust of wind, just 1,300m (0.8mi) from the start made it keel over. Eye witnesses experienced

the maiden voyages as follows: "When the ship reached the bay by Tegelviken, it gathered more wind in its sails and soon began to heel windward, righted itself again until it went full side down off Beckholmen and water gushed in through the gun portals, so that it slowly began to sink with raised sails, flags and all." At least 30 men drowned.

Majestic Error

Flashback: In 1625, around 1,000 oaks were cut down in the woods of Södermannland and the wood was transported to the Blasieholmen peninsula in what is today's Norrmalm district of Stockholm. In the following three years, carpenters, smiths and sailmakers worked on the new **flagship of the fleet,** a vessel which was very impressive for the time: 69m (226ft) long, 11.7m (38.4ft) wide and with a 52.5m (172ft) high mast. 64 cannons and a crew of 445 men was intended to make every enemy tremble in his shoes. However, it was only possible to fulfil the requirements of the king with a second cannon deck – a fatal alteration to the plan since at the beginning of the construction phase, the proportions of the ship had only been calculated on the basis of a single cannon deck. However,

The shipwreck can be observed from galleries close by

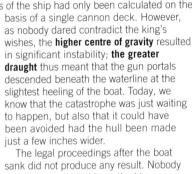

as nobody dared contradict the king's wishes, the **higher centre of gravity** resulted in significant instability; **the greater draught** thus meant that the gun portals descended beneath the waterline at the slightest heeling of the boat. Today, we know that the catastrophe was just waiting to happen, but also that it could have been avoided had the hull been made just a few inches wider.

The legal proceedings after the boat sank did not produce any result. Nobody had the courage to blame the king.

Salvaging the Boat

Many unsuccessful attempts were made to salvage the boat, only the cannons were saved relatively quickly. It was not until April 1961 that it was finally possible to salvage the wreck, but it would last until 1990 before the first visitors could admire the battleship in its own museum. Years of work were needed to conserve the wood and put the puzzle of **14,000 pieces** back together again. And even now the conservation of the *Vasa* still causes skilled craftsmen a headache. Over the centuries that the ship was under water a lot of sulphur penetrated the wood, which now in combination with the air becomes sulphuric acid and damages the wood.

The King's Titanic

You don't have to be boat enthusiasts to find this museum fascinating. Over several levels, the impressive building surrounds the around 50m (164ft) high *Vasa* battleship, which sank in 1628 on its maiden voyage and was almost totally salvaged, preserved and restored 300 years later. The most-visited museum in Scandinavia, Vasamuseet gives visitors insight into shipbuilding and the life of people in the 17th century.

❶ **Vasa:** The centrepiece of the museum is the salvaged and restored wreck of the *Vasa*, one of the largest warships of its time: 69m (226ft) long, 11.7m (38.4ft) wide and 52.5m (172ft) to the top of the mast. It could have carried 445 men, 145 of which would have been crew, the rest soldiers. There were women among the 30 bodies recovered.

❷ **Rig:** the rig was reconstructed using models from the 17th century.

❸ **Hull:** the hull of the ship contained 120t stones as ballast. This weight was not enough, however, to maintain the stability of the two-storey superstructure with the excessively heavy cannons.

❹ **Shipyard:** 400 people worked on the *Vasa* for three years. A number of models illustrate the building phases.

❺ **Ships in Battle:** A film shows what a sea battle would have been like in the 17th century. From this level, you reach the outside area and the icebreaker *Sankt Erik* and the lightship *Finngrundet*.

❻ **Life on Board:** Models provide an idea of the inside of the *Vasa*, which cannot be entered itself. At that time the captain's cabin was very luxurious, a stark contrast with the hard life of the crew, who had to sleep on deck and suffered from scurvy and hunger. Spoons, plates, coins, even a game of backgammon were found on the *Vasa*.

❼ **On the High Seas:** On this floor, you will learn how people sailed and navigated in the 17th century.

The decorative statues used to be painted in bright colours

A model of the *Vasa* shows the ship with its sails set

Vasamuseet

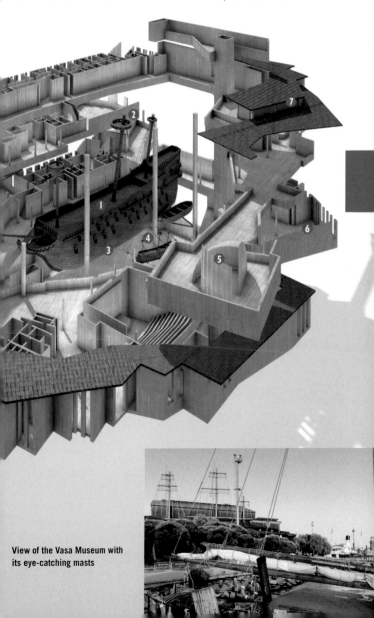

View of the Vasa Museum with its eye-catching masts

Djurgården, Skeppsholmen & Kastellholmen

The oak hull was not as dark as it appears today when it was put into the water. The *Vasa* was not only a "battleship" it was a **floating palace** that was intended to glorify the power of the king. That was the reason for the many hundreds of sculptures. lions, Biblical heroes, Roman emperors, marine animals and Greek gods. Today, they look very sombre, but they were once painted with bright colours, which against the red background would have looked very effective.

In its darkened hall, the "Vasa" looks very mystical; on the **galleries,** you can have a close look at the entire hull of the ship. The **figurehead** on the bow shows a 4m (13ft) jumping lion. This is also in homage to King Gustav II Adolf who was also known as the "Lion of the North".

TAKING A BREAK

From the **Museum restaurant,** you have a fantastic view out across the water and Skeppsholmen Island. In the summer, the terrace is a good place to watch the ships going by. The inexpensive lunch menu has a choice of different dishes every day, although one traditional Swedish favourite is served every day: *köttbullar med gräddsås, rårörda lingon och pressgurka* (meatballs with a cream sauce, cranberries and pressed cucumber).

The Estonia Monument bears the names of all those who died when the ship went down

➕ 182 C4   ✉ Galärvarvsvägen 14
☎ 08 51 95 48 00; www.vasamuseet.se
🕐 June–Aug daily. 8.30–6pm, otherwise 10am–5pm, Wed till 8pm
🚌 44, 47 H7   🎟 kr130

INSIDER INFO

- Anchored directly behind the museum in **Wasahamnen** (harbour) are veteran vessels that belong to the Maritime Museum: the icebreaker *Sankt Erik* (1915), the fast torpedo boat *Spica* (1966), the rescue ship *Bernhard Ingelsson* (1944) and the lightship *Finngrundet* (1903).
- A small way inland and you will come to the **Galärvarvskyrkogården**, a cemetery with a small chapel. This is where twelve crew members of the *Vasa* are buried.
- Very near the cemetery is the **Estonia Monument**, which commemorates the sinking of the *Estonia*. On 28 September 1994, the vessel sank on the way from Tallinn to Stockholm for reasons that have never been wholly established. More than 850 drowned, only 137 survived the catastrophe. The monument consists of three granite walls symbolising a ship's bow in which the names of the victims are engraved.

⭐3 Skansen

Skansen, one of the oldest open-air museums in the world, brings together in one location the typical dwellings, farmsteads and workshops found throughout Sweden. It is a vibrant museum with lots of different activities in the museum buildings that demonstrate traditional customs and handicrafts.

One of the 160 buildings: the traditional wooden Seglora Church

Artur Hazelius was a philologist and ethnographer, but he was also an enthusiastic collector. He initially collected Swedish traditional costumes that provided the foundation for the Nordic Museum (▶ 119). It was later that he discovered his passion for old farmsteads. He bought various buildings and had them reconstructed on a hill on the island of Djurgården. They provided the nucleus of the Skansen Open-Air Museum that was opened on the instigation of Hazelius in 1891. Until his death, he lived in a house in Skansen, and he is also found his last resting place there.

A Dynamic Museum

The Stockholmers received his idea with enthusiasm. The museum captured the mood of the national romantic trends and developed into a lively place in which rural traditions were experienced as opposed to being shown in sterile vitrines. Right from the start, Hazelius not only wanted to show the visitors rural life, he also wanted to present Scandinavia's animal world, which is why he had a reindeer enclosure set up in an area used for storing seed. Gradually, a 🐾 **zoo** developed, which houses around 300 animals from the Nordic region, including wolves, lynx, wolverine, brown bears and elk.

Enthusiasm for the establishment continues to be high. Skanset is not only a popular tourist goal but also a place in which Stockholmers celebrate traditional festivals or just enjoy a Sunday out with the family. Anyone who visits the museum should plan a whole day for it and be able to walk around easily. More than 160 buildings from the various regions of Sweden are spread out over the around 30ha (74 acres) of the museum. Most of the buildings are from the 18th, 19th and 20th centuries and provide insight into the different social classes of past times.

In the beautiful interior of the Seglora Church, you can admire the magnificent wooden pulpit

Insider Tip

The Old Town District

The houses from the reconstructed city district come from Stockholm's city district Södermalm and were originally erected in the 18th and 19th century. Wandering through the narrow alleyways is like going back in time through Sweden's history. Residential houses stand shoulder to shoulder with herbalists, bakers, glassworks, potteries, carpenters, printers, plumbers and other **small craft workshops**.

Insider Tip

The weekend is the best time to go. That's when flagons and dishes are made in the same way that they were 100 years ago, while at the bookbinders the hand-printed pages of a book are bound together. And at the goldsmiths, the bakery and the glass works, visitors are also shown the methods used for these old handcrafts.

Farms and Churches

The typical North Swedish farm **Älvrosgården** from the beginning of the 19th century consists of several buildings. Here you learn how people worked on the farm, how they spun wool and dried cheese, why people slept semi-seated and how toys used to be made.

Delsbogården from the Dalarna province was once an affluent agricultural business. Both houses are furnished with magnificent woodwork and paintings, wonderful hand-painted decorations adorn the walls.

The **Seglora Church** from 1729 moved to Skansen in 1916. The wooden building is painted in the typical oxblood red colour, the interior walls are plain white. A lot of Stockholmers get married here, and baptisms and confirmations also take part in the little wooden church.

The highest building on the museum premises is the **bell tower from Hälestad**, a small hamlet in Östergötland (East Gothland). The custom of putting bells in a free-standing tower has a long tradition in the north of Europe; it was only to save costs that they were later put into the church tower.

TAKING A BREAK

There are a lot of restaurants that cater for creature comforts. In the bright **Skansen Terrassen** you will find inexpensive lunch menus, also including *köttbullar*. In **Sollidens Restaurang** you can order a typical Swedish *smörgåsbord*, available from June–Aug every day from noon–4pm.

In the Skansen Open-Air Museum, you can learn about some of the wonderful Swedish traditions

🚻 183 D2   ✉ Djurgårdsslätten
☎ 08 4 42 80 00; www.skansen.se
🕙 Park: Jan–March and Oct–Dec Mon–Fri 10am–3pm, Sat, Sun 10am–4pm, April daily 10am–4pm, May–midsummer and Sep daily 10am–6pm, midsummer–end Aug daily 10am–8pm; houses, gardens, activities: May–Sep daily 11am–5pm or longer, Oct–April daily 11am–3pm G44 H7
💰 Depending on the time of year kr100–kr180

INSIDER INFO

■ If you walk a few hundred metres south from the main entrance, you come to the little island of **Beckholmen**. From the hill there, you can look down on the 19th-century dry docks that were cut into the bedrock and enjoy the maritime flair.

■ Every Tuesday evening several thousand Stockholmers make their way to Skansen to sing together (further information about Allsång på Skansen; ➤ 19).

Insider Tip

■ **Traditional festivals** such as Midsummer's Eve and The Lucia Procession are celebrated with particular gusto in Skansen. Before Christmas, a large market takes place here. There is a great view of the town from Sollidenplan, and it is a good place to enjoy the New Year.

■ From April–August, it is possible to travel in comfort from the Hazelius entrance to the museum hill with the **old rack railway.**

⭐6 ABBA The Museum

After quite a few years' planning and a failed first start, the time was eventually right in the early summer of 2013: ABBA one of the most successful pop groups in the world has now received its own museum. ABBA The Museum, as the exhibition is called, has become a popular tourist attraction and one of the most-visited sights in the country.

Waterloo marked the end for Napoleon. For ABBA, it was the beginning of their international career. In 1974, the four Swedes won the Eurovision Song Contest with this song. While quite a lot of other singers soon sink back into oblivion, ABBA firmly established themselves in the pop charts. The group is estimated to have sold 360 million sound recordings – only the Beatles Elvis and Michael Jackson have sold more. And their musical *Mamma Mia!* was not only shown at theatres around the globe, it was also successfully filmed.

ABBA is not just any old band. Agnetha, Benny, Björn and Anni-Frid are part of the cultural heritage – and as such have earned their very own 🛖 **museum**. It took long enough until the dream became reality. The original plans for the museum to open in 2009 came to nothing. What remained were a few million crowns debt that, in the end, the Swedish taxpayer had to pay.

Today, the guests are awaiting the four ABBAs at the Stockholm airport. Just as wax figures, but all the same. Arlanda calls itself "the official airport of the ABBA museum".

Stage Costumes and Gold Records

Agnetha, Benny, Björn and Anni-Frid donated records, instruments and many other mementoes to the museum. You can also see all the gold records that the band has won.

The gaudy **stage costumes** from the 1970s are a real eye-catcher. In their scanty shorts and miniskirts, Agnetha Fältskog and Anni-Frid Lyngstad turned the heads of almost every pubescent lad in Europe. Many a father wandering through the museum will smile to himself as he thinks back to the time that he wall-papered his teenager rooms with ABBA posters.

The museum shows almost everything that a fan can hope for. There is hardly a question about the group, which to the delight of the public really does comprise of two "real couples", that remains unanswered. There is even a copy of the band's holiday home here, including the original views out across the sea – recorded on video. Part of the, in comparison, normal programme includes being able to watch recordings of major concerts and admire the numerous awards that the group received year after year.

Benny, Björn, Anni-Frid and Agnetha welcome visitors at the entrance to the museum

In view of the continuing sales of CDs, videos and records, ABBA would probably still be able to walk on stage to full auditoriums, were it not for the fact their once much publicised perfect relationships fell apart. Agnetha Fältskog was married to Björn Ulveaus, Benny Andersson to Anni-Frid Lyngstad. When both marriages collapsed at the peak of their singing careers, it was downhill for ABBA as a group as well. The four persevered for a while, pretending that the harmony was still there during their performances. Eventually, though, in December 1982, the four announced the end of ABBA.

The museum also shows the decline of the quartet, albeit in significantly less detail than it portrays the successful times. That is probably what the fans would want. Even today, many still regret the personal Waterloo of Sweden's most well-known stars.

Bright and glittering costumes were ABBA's trademark – but how does anyone dance in those shoes?

➕ 182 C3

✉ Djurgårdsvägen 68 (besides the Gröna Lund leisure park)

☎ 07 71 75 75 75; www.abbathemuseum.com

🕐 May–Aug daily 10am–8pm, otherwise daily 10am–6pm, Wed, Thu until 8pm (last admission 90 min. before closure)

🚌 44 🚊 7 ⛴ Djurgårdsfärjan

🎟 kr195 (incl. admission for Swedish Music Hall of Fame in the same building; it is possible to book tickets online).

INSIDER INFO

If you wish, you can try your hand as the **fifth member of ABBA**, go up on stage and – technology makes it possible – perform *Dancing Queen*, *Mamma Mia* or one of the other unforgettable hits with the stars.

⭐ Waldemarsudde

In a wonderful location on the peninsula of Waldemarsudde, Prince Eugen, Duke of Närke, had a stately villa built overlooking the water. Here, he indulged his passions for painting and landscape gardening. In the house and park are paintings and sculptures from the Prince's estate.

Prince Eugen (1865–1947) was the youngest son of King Oscar II and his wife Sophia of Nassau. From an early age, he was more interested in art than in his royal duties. It was thus a logical step to study art, initially in Uppsala, then in Paris, whereby his greatest passion was landscape painting. He painted in Sörmland and Scania as well as in the surroundings of Stockholm, but also created the altarpiece in Kiruna Church, the frescoes in the Stockholm City Hall and the murals in the opera house. In Sweden, he became a renowned artist, but outside of Sweden, he remained relatively unknown.

The prince's villa dominates the peninsula, which is now also called Prince Eugen's Waldemarsudde

Painter and Art Collector
Prince Eugen fell in love with the Waldemarsudde peninsula on Djurgården very early on. In 1899 he eventually bought

a large piece of land. Together with the architect Ferdinand Boberg, he designed a palatial house in Art Nouveau style, which was extended with a modern atelier building about ten years later. When his villa was finished, he lived and painted in Waldemarsudde.

Besides painting, the prince was also a passionate art collector and great patron of the arts. When he died, his **art collection** comprised of several thousand paintings, sculptures and drawings, mainly by 19th and 20th century Swedish artists such as Bruno Liljefors, Richard Bergh, Anders Zorn, Karl Nordström and Ernst Josephsson. The rooms on the ground floor still have their original furnishings; the upper floors from the former atelier of the prince mainly provide the space for temporary exhibitions. Many of Prince Eugen's works, such as *Spring* and *The Cloud* are now on view in the house that he bequeathed to the state.

Park and Garden

The prince laid out the park and garden, from which there is a beautiful view of the water, with a lot of love and expertise. Between the vibrant, colourful flowerbeds, you can admire his **sculpture collection**, which include a copy of *Nike of Samothrace* from the Louvre, Auguste Rodin's *The Thinker* as well as Carl Milles' works *Archer* and *Triton*.

The prince's grave is behind the 18th-century Gamla huset (old house).

TAKING A BREAK

The light and friendly museum restaurant Prinsens kök serves lunch, soups, salads *smörgåsar* and other delicious snacks. When the weather is good, you can also look for a spot to have a picnic – either on one of the park benches or, better still, on the banks of the river.

🔛 183 F2 ✉ Prins Eugens väg 6
☎ 08 54 58 37 00; www.waldemarsudde.se
🕐 Tue–Sun 11am–5pm, Thu until 8pm, Park open all year round H7
💰 kr120

INSIDER INFO

■ From mid-June till the end of August **museum trams** also run every day on line 7N, otherwise only at the weekend. All of the vintage trams start at Norrmalmstorg and continue to Skansen; the café trams, which generally run every half an hour, go to Waldemarsudde. The tickets are available at the normal price; for information see www.djurgardslinjen.se/en.

■ In the **museum shop** you can purchase high-quality reproductions – but only of works by the artist-prince.

■ A pretty, around 45-minute **walk** – some of it by the water, some of it through a wood – takes you to Thielska Galleriet (➤ 124).

㉟ Moderna Museet
(The Museum of Modern Art)

The Museum of Modern Art can look back on a long history. It started in a former drill hall on Skeppsholmen, where it was housed from 1958 to 1998. The museum has stayed on the island, but it now resides in a building designed by Catalan architect Rafael Moneo.

The museum may look rather inconspicuous from the outside, but its collection – paintings sculptures, watercolours, drawings and photographs – is ranked among the best in Northern Europe. Especially for the **top-class temporary exhibitions**, which take place several times a year, it is often necessary to join a long queue in front of the entrance. The **permanent exhibition** bears the title *In our time* and provides a chronological overview of art from the 20th century to the present day – part of the museum concept being that the visitors first see the contemporary work and then go 100 years back in time.

High-calibre contemporary art awaits visitors in the Moderna museet

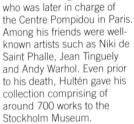

From Picasso to Dalí
From 1960, the engine behind the success was the art collector and director **Pontus Hultén**, who was regarded as one of the most influential exhibition organisers and who was later in charge of the Centre Pompidou in Paris. Among his friends were well-known artists such as Niki de Saint Phalle, Jean Tinguely and Andy Warhol. Even prior to his death, Hultén gave his collection comprising of around 700 works to the Stockholm Museum.

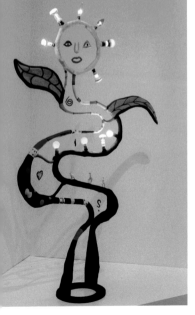

Today, the museum has in its possession 6,000 paintings, sculptures and installations, 25,000 watercolours, drawings and prints, 400 videos and 100,000 photographs. Swedish and other North-European artists make up the core of the permanent collection, but international masters, such as Pablo Picasso, Ljubov Popova, Salvador Dalí, Meret Oppenheim, Robert Rauschenberg, Donald Judd and Irving Penn are also represented.

Arkitektur- och designcentrum (Architecture Museum)

The small architecture museum next door provides information about Swedish architecture, from the first long houses of the Vikings to the typical Swedish houses made of wood and modern residential areas. The architectural styles are mainly communicated through true-to-scale models and drawings. The website provides information about the current exhibitions.

Since 1998, the Museum of Modern Art has been accommodated in a new building designed by Rafael Moneo

TAKING A BREAK

Refreshments are available at the **Moderna museet restaurant**. Chef Malin Södergren offers good lunches and delicious snacks. At the weekend, the brunch price is almost unbeatable – and includes one of the best views of Stockholm.

 Insider Tip

✚ 182 b3

Museum of Modern Art

✉ Skeppsholmen, Exercisplan 4 ☎ 08 52 02 35 00; www.modernamuseet.se,
🕐 Tue 10am–8pm, Wed–Sun 10am–6pm 🚌 65 ⛴ Djurgårdsfärjan
💲 Permanent exhibitions free, temporary exhibitions vary

Architecture Museum

✉ Skeppsholmen, Exercisplan 4 ☎ 08 52 02 35 00; www.arkdes.se
🕐 Tue 11am–7:30pm, Wed–Sun until 5:30pm 🚌 65 ⛴ Djurgårdsfärjan 💲 Free

INSIDER INFO

Insider Tip

The **Sculpture Park** of the Moderna museet is worth a visit. You can't miss the 16 colourful fantasy figures that Niki de Saint Phalle and Jean Tinguely created for the 1972 World Exhibition in Montreal. Not far away is the monumental mobile sculpture *The Four Elements* by Alexander Calder. Pablo Picasso contributed to the idea for the betograve figures *Frukost i de gröna* in the museum garden; the sculptures were created by the Norwegian artist Carl Nesjar.

36 Nordiska Museet
(Nordic Museum)

The imposing Nordic Museum resembles a castle. Stretching along 125m (410ft) and with numerous little turrets, this impressive building is on the island of Djurgården. The museum was founded at the end of the 19th century by Artur Hazelius; he also founded the nearby Skansen Open-Air Museum (➤ 109).

Hazelius started with his Scandinavian Ethnographic Collection in Drottningsgatan. In 1907, on completion of the museum, built **in National Romantic style** according to the plans of Isak Gustaf Clason, the collection was moved to Djurgården. From then on, the museum was called the Nordiska museet and became a foundation for the Swedish population.

Under the Gaze of Gustav Vasa

When you enter the museum, you find yourself in the over 20m (65ft) high **Central Hall**, where you can almost believe that you are in a church. The central exhibit is equally monumental: a 6m (19.7ft) high, colourfully painted and gilded **wooden statue of King Gustav I Vasa** by Carl Milles, probably Sweden's best-known sculptor. Visitors start their tour of the museum, which covers all facets of the country's cultural history, under the stern gaze of the king. The exciting journey through time starts in 1521, the year that Gustav I Vasa ascended to the throne, and ends in the present.

The cultural treasures of the Nordic Museum have a home fit for a king

Djurgården, Skeppsholmen & Kastellholmen

Daily Life in Changing Times

The ground floor is reserved for temporary exhibitions. On the three upper floors, visitors can examine all those things regarded as typical for Sweden over the last 500 years: including meticulously planned table arrangements, doll's houses, clocks, tobacco tins, costumes, painted farmhouse cupboards, furnished rooms as well as everyday objects and paintings. The exhibition provides information about traditions, customs and festivals. Among other things, visitors learn how Swedes celebrated Midsummer's Eve or Walpurgis Night. Individual ethnic groups are not forgotten either. Of particular interest is an especially interesting section dealing with the life, history and identity of the **Sami (Lapps)**, whose homeland stretched over the four countries of Sweden, Norway, Finland and Russia.

> **MULTITALENT**
> Did you know that Sweden's most famous playwright, August Strindberg, was also an artist? The museum shows some of his paintings.

Looking majestic and also a little fearsome: Gustav I Vasa, King of Sweden, receives visitors to the museum

TAKING A BREAK

Walk a few paces to the **Sjöcaféet** (▶ 130) on the Djurgården Bridge: You can eat a light meal directly by the water and afterwards paddle through the water in a canoe or kayak.

➕ 182 C4 ✉ Djurgårdsvägen 6–16
☎ 08 51 95 46 00; www.nordiskamuseet.se
🕐 June–Sep daily 9am–6pm, otherwise 10am–5pm, Wed until 8pm
🚌 44, 47 🚊 7 ⛴ Djurgårdsfärjan 🎫 kr100

INSIDER INFO

Those with a bit more time can stop off in **Lusthusportens park**, which is not far from Nordiska museet to the east of Djurgården Bridge. You enter it through a blue door with golden embellishments. A walk takes you along the water to **Villa Godthem** (Rosendalsvägen 9); the enchanting garden café offers light refreshment.

37 Museiparken (Museum Park)

It is easy to spend a whole day in the Museum Park in Ladugårdsgärdet; the park contains five different museums: The Museum of Ethnography, The National Museum of Science and Technology and the Maritime Museum rank among the museum highlights of Stockholm, whilst the Police Museum and National Sports Museum are more for extremely keen museum-goers.

You can also see this totem pole in the garden of the Museum of Ethnography

Since 1980 the **Etnografiska museet (Museum of Ethnography)** has been housed in the prize-winning, Falun red building by Jan Gazelius in the Museum Park. On the upper floor, the permanent exhibitions are dedicated mainly to North America, North and Central Africa, India, Japan and Mongolia. The ground floor is used for the temporary exhibitions. Also on view are the artefacts that the famous Swedish research travellers Sven Hedin and Carl von Linné brought back home from their expeditions. The North American Indians and their way of life are a central theme, particularly the time period from Columbus to the present day.

The **repository**, containing around 6,000 of the around 440,000 artefacts to be seen in the museum, offers a fascinating view behind the scenes. Here, everyone can go off on a discovery tour and feel like they are in a treasure chamber. Insider Tip

In the museum's garden, there is a **Japanese teahouse** in which tea ceremonies regularly take place during the summer.

For Technology Fans of All Ages

The **Tekniska museet (The National Museum of Science and Technology)** is the country's largest scientific museum and offers enough distractions to fill an entire day. On the ground floor is the machine hall, in which combustion engines, mining machinery, airplanes and vintage cars are on show. In the **Teknorama** children, adolescents and adults can perform experiments to their heart's content (all of the stations are described in English). On the upper floor, a large model railway from the 1950s makes children's dreams come true.

One of the most entertaining exhibitions shows what are claimed to be the **100 most important discoveries** of all time. This hitlist contains such diverse objects as wind

turbines, Tetra Pak, shoes, satellites, the compass, railway, money, the bicycle, CD and the car. This hitlist is the product of a representative survey that was carried out in Sweden. If you are not in agreement with the list, you can vote for your own favourite.

Those who still have the time and inclination can watch a film in the 4D cinema, which is not only three dimensional but where the seats also move, and scents of what the viewer is seeing also pervade the auditorium.

Besides the permanent exhibitions, Tekniska museet also organises temporary exhibitions on topical current issues.

Explorers of all ages will enjoy a visit to the National Museum of Science and Technology

For Real Sea Dogs

The **Sjöhistoriska museet (Maritime Museum)** shows exhibits on underwater archaeology, naval history and the original stern castle of King Gustav III's schooner *Amphion*. A whole room is dedicated to a collection of detailed models of boats down the ages. Every type of vessel from the Viking boats to the oil tanker are on view here in a miniature version. One of the largest exhibitions focuses on the topic of "Shipping & Shopping"; it shows that without the freight traffic on the world seas there would be no modern consumer society. To ensure that nobody gets bored, this exhibition has attached a great deal of importance to including interactive exhibits.

The **antique globes**, some of which date back to the 17th century, are wonderful artworks. The older ones only show a few white areas on the Earth's surface – Australia and large sections of North America were still not mapped at that stage. The same applies for the nautical charts that are also on show in the collection. A map by the Arab cartographer Al-Idrisi, only charts Europe, Asia and North Africa.

Still got some time? Then you can visit the **Polismuseet (Police Museum)** and learn all about the Swedish police force and at the **Riksidrottsmuseet (National Sports Museum)** everything about the development of sport in Sweden from the Olympic Games in 1912 to the present. Football fans can also watch matches between Sweden and other football nations.

Museiparken

TAKING A BREAK

The **Matmekka** restaurant in the Museum of Ethnography
has perfectly mastered the art of how to whisk its guests
off on a culinary world trip with fresh regional ingredients
and exotic spices. A particularly good choice for lunch
(open from 11am).

Museum of Ethnography
➕ 183 F5 ✉ Djurgårdsbrunnsvägen 34
☎ 010 4 56 12 99; www.varldskulturmuseerna.se/etnografiskamuseet
🕒 Tue–Sun 11am–5pm, Wed until 8pm 🚌 69 💶 Free

National Museum of Science and Technology
➕ 183 F4 ✉ Museivägen 7
☎ 08 4 50 56 00; www.tekniskamuseet.se
🕒 Daily 10am–5pm, Wed until 8pm 🚌 69 💶 kr150

Maritime Museum
➕ 183 E5 ✉ Djurgårdsbrunnsvägen 24
☎ 08 51 95 49 20; www.sjohistoriska.se
🕒 Tue–Sun 10am–5pm 🚌 69 💶 Free

Police Museum
➕ 183 F5 ✉ Museivägen 7
☎ 010 5 63 80 00; www.polismuseet.se
🕒 Tue–Fri noon–5pm, Sat, Sun 11am–5pm 🚌 69 💶 kr60

National Sports Museum
➕ 183 F5 ✉ Djurgårdsbrunnsvägen 26
☎ 08 6 99 60 10; www.riksidrottsmuseet.se
🕒 Tue–Fri noon–5pm, Sat, Sun 11am–5pm 🚌 69 💶 Free

Sea dogs should head for the Maritime Museum

INSIDER INFO

From the Museum park it is not far to the **Kaknästornet** (➤ 129). Go to the top of the
tower if the weather is good and treat yourself to a view over Stockholm.

㊳ Thielska Galleriet
(Thiel Gallery)

In 1896 Ernest Thiel bought his first larger painting *Morgonstämning vid havet (Morning Mood by the Sea)* by Bruno Liljefors. This was the beginning of a lifelong passion for collecting art that would eventually eat up his entire fortune.

Soon his flat on the Stockholmer Strandvägen became too small for the painting collection. He thus wrote a letter to a friend who was an architect, Ferdinand Boberg, expressing his wish to acquire a house that would enable him to be able to hang all of his paintings on the wall. Thiel was – at the time – still a successful, wealthy banker who could well afford to fulfil such a wish. So it was that in 1904 his dream house, a large white villa with green glazed tiles that combined Moorish splendour, European Art Nouveau and Swedish manor house tradition appeared on the highest point in the eastern part of Djurgården island. And as Thiel had wanted, there were two large rooms on the upper floor which were reserved exclusively for his art collection.

Ernest Thiel, portrait by Edvard Munch

From Millionaire to Bankrupt
The passionate art collector was close friends with many Scandinavian artists of his time. This illustrious circle included Eugène Jansson, Carl Larsson and Bruno Liljefors; even Edvard Munch visited him on a number of occasions. Initially Ernest Thiel had enough funds to buy the many paintings, but after only 15 years one of the richest men in Sweden had spent his entire fortune

and manoeuvred himself into serious financial difficulties. In order to save his art collection, the Swedish state took it over in 1924. Two years later it was opened up to the public.

After a number of unsuccessful renovation attempts, the residence has now regained its original appearance. The Thielska Galleriet now owns **one of the most important collections of North European art** from the later 19th century to early 20th century.

From Carl Larsson to Edvard Munch

The highlights of the Thiel Gallery's collection of Swedish artists include the light, friendly paintings of Carl Larsson from Sundborn and the, in part, large-format landscapes of Bruno Liljefors. Thiel did not only acquire the works of Swedish artists though, the Norwegian Edward Munch is also represented here with eleven pictures, including *The Sick Child*, *Despair* and *Girls on the Bridge*; the tower room also contains some of his graphic reproductions. Ernest Thiel was particularly proud of these acquisitions, totally convinced that his Munch Room was unique in Europe. On the top floor of the gallery is the Death Mask of Friedrich Nietzsche, whose books Thiel had not only read but in some cases translated.

A walk across the **park-like grounds** is also well worthwhile. Here you will find works by well-known sculptors like Auguste Rodin and Gustav Vigeland. Ernest Thiel's ashes were buried under Rodin's sculpture *L'ombre (The Shadow)*.

Insider Tip

TAKING A BREAK

Monika Ahlberg runs the little **museum café**. She is a well-known author in Sweden and has written many cookery books, and she often has programmes on the radio and television. Her menu offers a small selection of lunch dishes and snacks. When the weather is nice, you can also sit in the sculpture garden. At the nearby eastern point of Djurgården is the **Café Blockhusporten**. Here you can sit directly by the water and watch the boats as you enjoy delicious snacks.

➕ 183 east. F3 ✉ Sjötullsbacken 8
☎ 08 6 62 58 84; www.thielska-galleriet.se
🕐 Tue–Sun noon–5pm, Thu until 8pm
🚌 69 🎫 kr100

INSIDER INFO

- When the weather is nice, it is worth walking around the **eastern tip** of Djurgården.
- The Sjövägen ferry line connects Djurgården (landing stage Blockhusodden, between Thielska Galleriet and Café Blockhusporten) with **Nacka Strand**, where one of the most spectacular works by the sculptor Carl Milles awaits you (▶ 157).

Djurgården, Skeppsholmen & Kastellholmen

At Your Leisure

The 19th-century castle gave the little island its name

39 Östasiatiska museet (East Asian Museum)

The museum founded in 1926 has **one of the most important collections of Chinese art** outside Asia. Johan Gunnar Andersson provided the basic stock of the collections on his expedition in the 1920s. He was allowed to export many prehistoric finds from China to Sweden. One of the most valuable exhibits is a painted ceramic head that is around 4,500 years old. The China Presentation is supplemented by a porcelain and literature collection. Other focuses of the museum are Japan, Korea and India. You can always look forward to the temporary exhibitions, which invariably present something special (for example the Chinese Terracotta Army was exhibited here).

The extended yellow museum building was built in the late 17th century by Nicodemus Tessin the Younger. It used to serve as ropemakers, poorhouse and stall.

🔲 182 A/B4 ✉ Tyghusplan, Skeppsholmen
🖥 www.varldskulturmuseerna.se/en/ostasiatiskamuseet
🕐 Tue 11am–8pm, Wed–Sun 11am–5pm
🚇 Kungsträdgården
🚌 65 🎫 Free

40 Skeppsholmen & Kastellholmen

A cast-iron bridge with a royal coat of arms on the balustrade connects the Norrmalm district with Skeppsholmen, from where you can also reach the smaller island of Kastellholmen over another bridge. Ferries operate between Skeppsholmen as well as Djurgården and Gamla Stan.

Owing to its favourable strategic position, **Skeppsholmen** island became a marine base in the mid-17th century. To ensure that the king could continue to enjoy a nice view, buildings facing the castle were built in an appropriately representative style. The best example is the red Admiralty Building with its turrets. On a hill and thus

visible for miles around is the Skeppsholmen Church, a neo-classical building with a circular dome that is reminiscent of the Pantheon in Rome. Nowadays, the building is only used as a concert hall. At the end of the 1960s, the navy moved out of Skeppsholmen; since then museums and cultural institutions have used the historical buildings.

Moored off the western shore of Skeppsholmen, the three-master *af Chapman* has found what is probably its last anchorage. The ship takes its name from the master shipbuilder Fredrik Henrik af Chapman, born in Gothenburg in 1721. Launched in 1888 in the English harbour of Whitehaven, this full-rigged ship can look back on a very diverse history; it has been a freight ship, training ship for the Swedish navy and was a barracks ship during World War II. Today it serves as an unusual and very popular youth hostel (➤ 38).

The small island of **Kastellholmen** practically comprises of nothing more than a big block of granite.

Since 1848, enthroned on its highest point is the castle resembling a medieval fort, which gave the island its name. A few residential houses, a small marina and a late 19th-century pavilion complete the list of buildings on the island.

In earlier times, the gentlemen belonging to the royal skating club met in the pavilion after they had done a few circuits round the island on their skates. Later the Royal Swedish Yacht Club took over the building, which is now part of the Skeppsholmen Hotel.
🚩 182 A4–B3 🚌 65

🔢🎪 Gröna Lund
Sweden's Oldest Amusement Park suffers from a lack of space, but that in no way diminishes its popularity. Everything began in 1883 when the German Jacob Schultheiss opened a small fairground here and named it after the favourite bar of Sweden's most popular bard Carl Michael Bellman "Gröna Lund". The amusement park is appealingly located next to the water and offers entertainment for the entire family. In the tightest of spaces, you will find big dippers, a Ferris wheel, a chain carrousel and many other rides. Besides the usual funfair attractions, there are also vaudeville shows and concerts at which international names take

In Gröna Lund's chain carousel, you literally fly over the water

Djurgården, Skeppsholmen & Kastellholmen

In the Junibacken Park, Pippi Longstocking, among others, tells of her adventures

part. Scores of restaurants cater for the well-being of the visitors.

➕ 182 C3 ✉ Lilla Allmänna Gränd 9
☎ 08 58 75 01 00; www.gronalund.com
🕐 end April–mid-Sep, changing opening times, mainly10am–10pm
🚌 44, 47 🚋 7 ⛴ Djurgårdsfärjan
💰 kr110, on concert evenings kr220

42 🍴 Aquaria vattenmuseet (Aquaria Water Museum)

The Aquaria Water Museum is divided into Rainforest, Mangrove, Tropical Ocean and Nordic Exhibits. The somewhat small museum uses every square metre, so visitors wander on convoluted paths through South American Rainforest, see piranhas and poison frogs, and can observe life under water from behind glass. One special exhibition area is dedicated to seahorses. In the **seawater aquarium** are moray eels, coral, starfish and sharks as well as a tropical coral riff with surgeonfish and sea urchins. Scandinavia's exhibits include a mountain lake in which Arctic char swim, as well as a salmon leap.

➕ 182 C3 ✉ Falkenbergsgatan 2
☎ 08 6 60 90 89; www.aquaria.se
🕐 mid-June–mid-Aug daily 10am–6pm, otherwise Tue–Sun 10am–4:30pm
🚌 44, 47 🚋 7 ⛴ Djurgårdsfärjan
💰 kr100

43 Liljevalchs konsthall (Liljevalch's Art Gallery)

Since its opening in 1916, this state art gallery financed by industrialist Carl Fredrik Liljevalch and built by architect Carl Bergsten in neo-classical style exhibits the work of young, still relatively unknown artists. Generally, four exhibitions take place each year, the most well-known of which is the **vårsalongen (Spring Exhibition)** from the end of January to the end of March.

Carl Milles' sculpture *The Archer* stands at the entrance to the art gallery on a tall granite column.

The art gallery has been undergoing renovation work, and until it is opened again the exhibitions are taking place in other locations (e.g. Nybrokajen 2 on Blasieholmen and Malmtorgsgatan 8 in Norrmalm, current info online).

➕ 182 C3 ✉ Djurgårdsvägen 60
☎ 08 50 83 13 30; www.liljevalchs.se
🚌 44, 47 🚋 7 ⛴ Djurgårdsfärjan

What is remarkable about the Stockholm television tower is its square floor plan

Rosendahl Palace – once a summer residence, now a museum

44 Junibacken

Here everything is about the most successful children's book author in the world, Astrid Lindgren, who was able to work on the amusement park during her lifetime. With the **"story train" Sagatåget**, visitors can explore the world of Pippi Longstocking. The classics by other children's book authors are also picked up in Junibacken. *Alfie Atkins* by Gunilla Bergström, the *Moomins* by Tove Jansson and *Pettson and Findus* by Sven Nordqvist. Presentations take place on the stage several times a day. The shop stocks children's toys and Astrid Lindgren classics.

➕ 182 B4 ✉ Galärvarvsvägen 8
☎ 08 58 72 30 00; www.junibacken.se
🕐 July–mid-Aug daily 10am–6pm, June and mid until end Aug daily 10am–5pm, otherwise Tue–Sun 10am–5pm
🚌 67, 69 🚋 7
⛴ Djurgårdsfärjan 💰 kr159

45 Rosendals slott (Rosendal Palace)

King Karl XIV Johan (1763–1844) commissioned architect Fredrik Blom with the building. Blom designed a summer residence in Empire style according to the monarch's wishes. Since 1913 it

has served as a museum that highlights the life and period of the man who commissioned it. The completely preserved interior design boasts magnificent furniture, carpets, textiles and artworks. A short detour takes you to **Rosendals Trädgård**, an organic market garden with a restaurant (➤ 130).

➕ 183 F4 ✉ Rosendalsvägen 49
☎ 08 4 02 61 30; www.kungahuset.se
🕐 June–Aug Tue–Sun only as part of 45-minute tours 11am, 1pm, 2pm, 3pm, Sep Sat, Sun 11am, 1pm, 2pm, 3pm
🚌 67 🚋 7 💰 kr100

46 Kaknästornet (The Kaknäs Tower)

North-east of the museum park in Ladugårdsgärdet stands the 155m (508ft)-high television tower that was erected in the 1960s. From the **viewing platform** at 128m (420ft), there is a magnificent view of Stockholm and the surroundings, including the skerries. The view from the panorama windows in the restaurant is also a treat.

➕ 183 east F5
✉ Mörka Kroken, Ladugårdsgärdet
☎ 08 6 67 21 05; www.kaknastornet.se
🕐 June–Aug Mon–Sat 9am–10pm, Sun 9am–6pm, otherwise shorter
🚌 69 💰 kr60

Where to... Eat and Drink

Prices
for a main course without drinks:
£ under kr200
££ kr200–kr350
£££ over kr350

Blå Porten £
Salmon, lamb and *köttbullar*, lunch with a Mediterranean touch and good cakes are the best argument for a break between visiting museums. You sit in a calm, green inner courtyard. It is popular with the Stockholmers.
🚏 182 C3 ✉ Djurgårdsvägen 64
☎ 08 6 63 87 59; www.blaporten.com
🕐 Daily 11am–7pm 🚌 44, 47

Flickorna Helin & Voltaire £
The specialities are bread, rolls and cakes from the restaurant's own bakery. Light meals, such as salads and sandwiches, are also available. The house looks like a pretty little castle; in the summer you can sit on the terrace, which is still bathed in the sun in the afternoon.
🚏 183 D4 ✉ Rosendalsvägen 14
☎ 08 6 64 51 08; www.helinvoltaire.com
🕐 Mon–Sat 9am–5pm, Sun 10am–5pm
🚌 67 🚋 7

Insider Tip

Kafé Kruthuset £
At the east end of Djurgården, you can enjoy the view of the skerry island Fjäderholmarna. The 17th-century power tower stands on the premises of a sailing club. Besides coffee, cake and light meals, you can also order *strömming* and *köttbullar*.
🚏 183 east F5 ✉ Hunduddsvägen
☎ 08 6 61 83 37; www.kafekruthuset.se
🕐 Wed–Sun 10am–5pm 🚌 69

Rosendals Trädgård £–££
Not far from the palace of the same name, Rosendal's gardens are beautifully kept, and fruit and vegetables are cultivated. One of the greenhouses houses a café, and in the summer you can also sit outside. The cakes and bread come from the inhouse bakery.
🚏 183 E4 ✉ Rosendalsterrassen 12
☎ 08 54 58 12 70; www.rosendalstradgard.se
🕐 May–Sep daily 11am–5pm, otherwise Tue–Sun 11am–4pm 🚌 44

Wärdshuset Ulla Winbladh ££
In this restaurant, you can order traditional Swedish fare of the more refined kind in a matching historical environment.
🚏 183 D4 ✉ Rosendalsvägen 8
☎ 08 53 48 97 01; www.ullawinbladh.se
🕐 Mon 11:30am–10pm, Tue–Fri 11:30am–11pm, Sat 12:30pm–11pm, Sun 12:30pm–10pm
🚌 44

Where to... Go Out

Sjöcaféet
Directly on the Djurgården Bridge you can eat lunch overlooking the water and then work it all off using the sporting facilities. The offer includes canoes, kayaks, bicycles and golf carts. In an historic boules hall, instructors will show you how to master this ancient game
🚏 182 C4 ✉ Galärvarvsvägen 2
☎ 08 6 60 57 57; www.sjocafeet.se
🕐 Daily 9am–9pm 🚋 7 ⛴ Djurgårdsfärjan

Cirkus
This gloriously nostalgic building was built for the circus in 1892. After various conversions, it is now the event site for concerts, musicals, shows, congresses and fairs.
🚏 183 D3 ✉ Djurgårdsslätten 43–45
☎ 08 6 60 10 20; www.cirkus.se 🚌 44

Södermalm

 **Little Treats**

Look over Stockholm

Regardless of whether from the SkyView gondola of the **Globen** (► 144) or from **Mosebacke's beer garden** (► 154) – a bird's eye view of the capital is always worthwhile!

Go for a Swim

The best beaches in the city centre are in the Södermalm area, for example on **Långholmen** (► 142).

Eat with Pippi Longstocking

That's not possible of course. But those who visit **Lasse i Parken** (► 151) will still think that they are in a Swedish fairy tale.

Södermalm

Getting Your Bearings

The former working-class district has metamorphosed into a trendy district in the last few years. Not only artists and other creative talents feel at home here, the upper middle class is increasingly moving in, which is gradually changing the social structures. The gentrification in Södermalm has also resulted in the not altogether unproblematic expulsion of the old inhabitants by the new, wealthier clientele.

Södermalm is known for its lively nightlife and also offers fun bars, clubs and pubs that are not in the city's renowned nightlife district of SoFo (► 136). Götgatan has developed into one of the city's main shopping boulevards; from the beer garden on the Mosebacke terrace (► 154), you have a wonderful view of Stockholm. The little alleys in the district around Mariaberget (► 148), which play an important part in the novels of Stieg Larsson, entice you to take a leisurely stroll. Situated along the Hornsgatspuckeln are some of the city's most interesting galleries. Theatre buffs will like the Södra Teatern by Mosebacke torg. Those who like swimming are spoilt for choice with the beaches here. The most beautiful one is at Långholmsbadet, where during the summer you can sunbathe either on the smooth rocks or in the sand.

Water sports in the centre of the capital: Stand-up paddling in the channel between Södermalm and Långholmen

Getting Your Bearings

View of the evening silhouette of Södermalm and Mariaberget

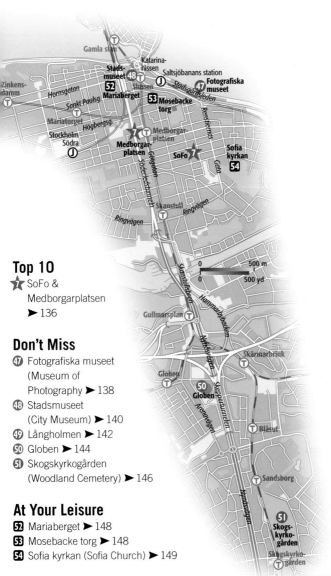

Top 10

⭐ SoFo &
Medborgarplatsen
► 136

Don't Miss

At Your Leisure

The Perfect Day

Whether you need one, two or even more days to tour Södermalm will depend on how easily you are tempted in by the many cafés and bars, and whether you are someone who likes shopping. If you only concentrate on the sights and resist all the other distractions, you will be able to take in the main sights in a day.

🕙 10:00am

Make a relaxed start to the tour through Södermalm with a walk through the 52 **Mariaberget** (► 148) district. Here you can wander along the picturesque alleys or browse the galleries on Hornsgatan. Don't miss the splendid panorama from the viewing platform at the end of Monteliusvägen.

🕚 11:00am

There is an equally beautiful view from the platform of the **Katarina Lift** (► 141).

In theory, it is possible to prepare for your city tour with a visit to the 48 **City Museum** (► 140). Anyone wishing to study the models of the town in more detail can of course shorten the following lunch break.

🕧 12:30pm

Now it is a difficult choice, either take time for (window) shopping or spend a bit more time over lunch? In Götgatan (left & right), on ⭐ **Medbogarplatsen** (► 137) as well as in

Folkungagatan and the adjoining streets, there is an enormous choice of restaurants and boutiques. Perfect for an inexpensive lunch break is the **String** (➤ 152) in Nytorgsgatan (no. 38). From here you can take a walk after the meal to **54** **Sofia Church** (➤ 149) and to the little picturesque wooden houses by the Vita Bergen.

🌐 2:30pm

The afternoon can be used for a trip to the Globen (Ericsson Globe) and Skogskyrkogården. It is up to you in which order you visit the two sights. First of all, you have to get there though. Strictly speaking, neither attraction is in Södermalm, and they would both be an extremely long walk, so you need to take a metro.

🌐 3:00pm

Don't miss the opportunity to whiz to the top of the **50** **Globen** (➤ 144) in a SkyView gondola. Again you are rewarded with a fascinating view of Stockholm – this time from a completely different perspective than from the observation platforms you visited in the morning.

🌐 4:30pm

What a contrast! The vast **51** **Woodland Cemetery** (➤ 146) has secured itself a place on UNESCO's list of World Heritage Sites with its exceptional garden architecture.

🌐 6:30pm

Back in the nightlife district of ⭐**SoFo** (➤ 136; above). In the traditional **Kvarnen** beer hall (➤ 150) in Tjärhovsgatan (no. 4), you can combine dinner with a visit to a literary location. It was here that the hero Mikael Blomkvist of crime writer Stieg Larsson's *Millennium* trilogy used to come on a regular basis.

🌐 11:00pm

Why not visit a museum at midnight? The **47** **Museum of Photography** (➤ 138) offers an opportunity to do just that: three days a week, it is open until 1am in the morning.

★ SoFo & Medborgarplatsen

A trendy district with a trendy name: For some years SoFo, the area south of Folkungagatan, has been the Stockholmers' favourite night-life district. Pubs, bars and restaurants, as well as boutiques and galleries pull in the crowds.

The district is bordered by the previously mentioned Folkungagatan in the north, Erstagatan in the east, Götgatan in the west and Ringvägen in the south. Apparently, the name was conceived by three local men who were on paternal leave and philosophising over a glass of wine at the time. Whether the anecdote is true, nobody can say. The fact is that "SoFo" is now so successful as a brand name that it has been registered with the Swedish Patent Office.

Pubs and Bars

Today, the district is the home of artists, designers and students – whereby the latter, owing to the once low rents, had already discovered the district for themselves long before it became hip. In the meantime, lawyers, doctors and professors find SoFo chic and have thus ensured that the days of affordable student flats are a thing of the past. A good mix of restaurants, cafés, galleries and boutiques has resulted in the meteoric rise of the district. Clustered

The north part of Götgatan is a pedestrian zone – full of tempting restaurants, bars and shops

in the area around the central square, **Nytorget**, are several culinary greats (➤ 151).

Medborgarplatsen

"Medis", as the locals call the square, is located on the edge of SoFo. With its discos, pubs and open-air cafés it offers a natural extension to the nightlife district. The square was set up in the mid-19th century during the construction of the (now subterranean) south station, which is why the square retained its original name Södra Bantorget (Southern Railway Square) for many years. It was not until the 1940s when the **Medborgarhus**, a sort of community centre, was built here that it received its present name.

In front of the entrance to Medborgarhus is a memorial to the Swedish Foreign Minister Anna Lindh, who was killed in 2003. She held her last speech here shortly before her death. A further monument on the square is **Kasper** – a clown thumbing his nose at the rich and powerful.

Söderhallarna, the district's market hall is also worth a stop. It is right next to the square (www.soderhallarna. com; most of the shops are open from 10am to 7pm). On the corner of Götgatan is the **Lillienhoffska palats** from 1670, which once belonged to an English minister and for that reason is called the Engelska huset (English House). Until 1888, the building was an almshouse, today it is home to the restaurant Snaps, a popular after-work meeting place.

Located not far from Medborgarplatsen, at no. 55 Götgatan, in a former cinema, you will find the musical theatre **Göta Lejon** (www.gotalejon.se). Until the beginning of the 20th century, the notorious **Restaurant Hamburg** was located here, in which condemned prisoners came to eat their last meal. The glasses from which they drank were kept and exhibited as gruesome souvenirs for visitors to the restaurant.

TAKING A BREAK

If you feel like something to nibble or even something more substantial, it is worth heading for **Söderhallarna** (➤ top), in which 20 restaurants and cafés offer a choice of dishes ranging from kebab to panini and sushi.

➕ 181 E/F1 🚇 Medborgarplatsen

INSIDER INFO

- A **list of all the shops, boutiques and galleries in SoFo** is available online at http://sofo-stockholm.se.
- At the **SoFo Night**, which takes place on the last Thursday of each month, all the shops are open until 9pm. Many attract the guests with live music and previews.
- On a **free tour through Södermalm**, you also get to known the SoFo district (www.freetourstockholm.se).

Södermalm

⁴⁷ Fotografiska Museet
(Museum of Photography)

The Museum of Photography is located on the bank of the Baltic Sea. Stockholm had to wait a long time for an exhibition space for the topic of photography. In the meantime, it is one of the most important museums of its kind worldwide.

The original plan was that the former Art Nouveau customs building, designed and built by the well-known Swedish architect Ferdinand Boberg between 1906 and 1910, would be used for the ABBA Museum. However, after these plans were scrapped, it became the new home of North Europe's largest Museum of Photography in 2010. This is the platform for four major and a good dozen smaller temporary exhibitions each year. These have included, among others, photographers of the ilk of Martin Schoeller, Robert Mapplethorpe, Nick Brandt, Annie Leibovitz and David Drebin. It is not very surprising that in the meantime the museum is one of the most visited sights in the city – more than 500,000 people come here each year to see the exhibited works.

On an exhibition area of around 2,500m² (27,000ft²), the Museum of Photography presents the works of well-known photographers

Fjällgatan Viewpoint
Using the **Söderbergs trappor**, the longest staircase in Stockholm's inner city (144 steps), you can walk up

from the Museum of Photography to the Fjällgatan viewpoint. At least at the moment you can. It is very likely, however, that the historic staircase will fall victim to the building work in the area by Slussen – currently a huge bus station, among other things, is under construction. At the top, you have a superb view of Stockholm from the Fjällgatan. The road is also a regular stop for the tour buses, which take a break here so that their guests can take a photo.

At no. 34 Fjällgatan is the small **Stigbergets Borgarrum** Museum in which a home from the 19th century has been preserved for posterity (open May and Sep–Dec each Sun 1pm–3pm).

Insider Tip

TAKING A BREAK

The restaurant and café on the top floor of the museum are more than just places that you quickly snack to quell the hunger pangs after visiting the exhibition. The ingredients for the inexpensive meals come from local organic farmers. The restaurant has already bagged a number of awards. The two eateries also win points for their wonderful view of Gamla Stan, the Royal Palace (▶ 80) and the Skeppsholmen Island, where the sailing vessel *af Chapman* (▶ 127) lies at anchor. Unusual: the museum even has its own bar.

The Fotografiska Museet is also very appealing on the outside

✚ 182 A2 ✉ Stadsgårdshamnen 22
☎ 08 50 90 05 00; www.fotografiska.eu
🕐 Sun–Wed 9am–9pm, Thu–Sat 9am–1Uhr
🚇 Slussen 🎫 kr120

INSIDER INFO

- Back to the museum after a visit to the bar? That is not a problem at Fotografiska. Three evenings a week, the museum is **open until 1am**.
- Do you want to improve your skills as a photographer? The Museum of Photography also organises courses.
- Every Friday at 6pm, 7pm and 8pm **free tours** are organised through the exhibition. Registration is not necessary. However, at the moment, the tours are only in Swedish.
- The **museum shop** offers more than the usual souvenirs. Here you can find one of the best selection of photography books in all of Stockholm. The only shop that has a comparable assortment is F-Concept on Sergels torg – and it, too, is also run by the Museum of Photography.

Insider Tip

㊽ Stadsmuseet
(City Museum)

With its exhibitions on city history, the City Museum offers the perfect introduction to every Stockholm visit. However, it is closed for renovation work till 2018. Until then, tourists can still book the excellent tours organised by the museum and enjoy the view from the Katarina Lift.

Stockholm's City Museum is close to the Slussen metro station. Like many of the 17th-century buildings in the city, it was built by Nicodemus Tessin the Elder. After its completion in 1663, it was initially the headquarters of an international trading company, then the town hall of Södermalm. As a result of a fire in 1680, the building was badly damaged; the son of the master builder, Nicodemus Tessin the Younger, took charge of the renovation work and had his father's building restored to its former glory.

Since the 1940s, it has housed the City Museum. The museum focuses very closely on the history of the city by, for instance, reproducing the development of Stockholm in the form of models of the town, At the same time, it does not lose sight of current developments. There is, for example, a detailed presentation of the Million Homes Programme (▶ 11), a post-war programme set up in order to build one million new residences in the space of ten years. Since 2015 and until November 2018, the

The Stockholm City Museum resides in the former Town Hall of Södermalm

A popular walk organised by the City Museum is "The Millennium Tour"

museum is closed for renovation work. Nonetheless, the events organised by the City Museum still take place – and these include the popular **city walks** "The Millennium Tour" and the "ABBA Tour" (information regarding the renovation work and city walks are on the internet).

Insider Tip

Katarinahissen

When the Katarina Lift, which goes from Slussplan up 39m (128ft) to Mosebacke, was opened in 1883, it developed in no time at all into a popular excursion. On average 1,500 passengers were transported for a fare of 5 öre to the top every day. In 1933, the original lift had to be replaced. Since 2011, the replacement has also ceased operation owing to technical problems. The lift was in such a bad condition that it was simply too dangerous to keep it in operation. The experts are not convinced that it is worth repairing.

Time and again, there are rumours that the Katarina Lift may soon be working again – but nothing has happened so far. Nonetheless, it is always worth making a stop here. You can still access the **viewing platform.** True, it is now necessary to climb up on foot, but the fantastic view makes it more than worthwhile.

Insider Tip

TAKING A BREAK

Treat yourself to a meal with a view. In the connecting bridge between the Katarina Lift and a neighbouring office building is the popular **Gondolen** restaurant (➤ 150). It has an inexpensive lunch menu for kr135.

🕂 181 E2   ⊠ Ryssgården
☎ 08 50 83 16 20; http://stadsmuseet.stockholm.se
🕐 Closed until 2018 for renovation purposes
Ⓜ Slussen   ⛴ Djurgårsfjärian

INSIDER INFO

- Just a few metres south of the City Museum is the house in which the poet and singer **Carl Michael Bellmann** (1740–1795) lived in the 1770s. Bellmann's drinking songs continue to be sung with great gusto at events where the mood is good and the drinks flow. The building is now a museum and can be viewed on the first Sunday of every month at 1pm during a tour (only available in Swedish; Urvädersgränd 3, admission kr100).
- The most **beautiful beer garden** in the town is by the nearby Mosebacke torg (➤ 154).

49 Långholmen

The approximately 1.5km (1mi) long and 400m (1,300ft) wide Långholmen north of Södermalm is very popular with the Stockholmers, especially during the summer. From 1880 to 1975, however, most of the "visitors" to the island had not chosen to go there and were in fact extremely loath to stay there. That was the time that there was a prison on the island, mainly inhabited by serious criminals.

Before the island was used as a prison, it was much narrower than it is today – and its distinctive shape was why people called it the "long island" (Swedish "Långholmen"). It was not until the prison was set up in the 19th century that the island was enlarged. To achieve that, the later inmates of the prison poured mud over the barren rock island.

Behind Swedish Curtains

There are a lot of spooky tales connected with Långholmen. For example, the one about Alfred Ander, who was the last convict to be executed in that prison in Sweden. The inn-keeper was known as a petty criminal. One cold January day in 1910, he decided to put an end to his constant money worries once and for all and rob a bank. The robbery did not go at all as planned. When the female cashier tried to stop Ander, he retaliated so brutally that she died shortly after the robbery. The police caught Ander and he was hung on 23 November.

After closing parts of the prison, the remaining buildings were converted into, among other things, a restaurant, a youth hostel and an inexpensive three-star hotel. The Swedish crime author Arne Dahl, who lives directly opposite the island, recommends people to book a single "cell" at Långholmen Hotel if they fancy getting an idea of what it is like to be a prisoner. He writes: "The cells have been given a fresh coat of paint. Yet, you don't need to be a crime author to be able to imagine what it was like to be an inmate

Unusual and not exactly luxurious: a single "cell" in the prison hotel on Långholmen

These days, Långholmen is a recreation area in the middle of the city

in this enclosed space, to imagine the loneliness, the fear and the rage. In my book *Musical Chairs* the prison is the setting for a sinister prison riot." Also offering a look inside the world of prisoners and the history of the prison is 🏛 Fängelsemuseum (Prison Museum).

Stockholm Summer Idyll

The second tour around the island in the 🏛 **Nature Recreation Area** that has developed around the former prison is far more gratifying. The elongated island is a favourite picnic and bathing destination of the Stockholmers. The walk around Långholmen, which provides beautiful views of Stadshuset (➤ 50), is also very popular.

TAKING A BREAK

On weekdays, Långholmens Wärdshus has a reasonably priced lunch menu for kr129 (tel: 08 7 20 85 50, Mon–Fri 11:30am–11pm, Sat noon–11pm, Sun noon–5pm).

✚ 180 a2/3 ✉ Långholmsmuren 20
☎ 08 7 20 25 00; www.langholmen.com 🚇 Hornstull

Prison Museum
🕐 Daily 11am–4pm 🎫 kr25

INSIDER INFO

The Prison Museum has put together a few activities, ranging from a simple tour of the prison to a **"Jailbreak"**, led by former inmates. If you wish to take part in any of these activities, you must book well in advance (information is available on the website).

㊿ Globen

When world stars come to Stockholm, they usually perform in the Ericsson Globe. The multipurpose hall in the Johanneshov district, which was built for the World Ice Hockey Championships, has space for up to 16,000 viewers.

The 85m (279ft) high, white dome measuring 110m (360ft) across is reminiscent from a distance of an oversized egg. It makes the Globe the largest spherical-shaped building in the world. Large events of all kinds – whether pop and rock concerts, ice hockey games or the Eurovision Song Contest – take place in the arena. Leading figures from politics and society who come to visit Stockholm also appear on stage here to speak to the Swedish public: Pope John Paul II held a mass at the Globe, Nelson Mandela and the Dalai Lama gave their speeches here.

Stockholm at your feet – the view from the Globen SkyView is breathtaking

Since February 2009, the Globe's official name has been the **Ericsson Globe**. That was when the Swedish telecommunications provider acquired the name rights for the arena.

🏛 SkyView

The latest attraction at the Globe is the SkyView. Since 2010, you can get into a **glass gondola** and zoom up on rails along the outside of the building to the highest point. A perfect view is guaranteed. The trip takes about 20 min; before you set off, the programme includes a 15 min film about the history of the Globen.

SkyView can rightly claim to be unique; it is the only place in the world that you can ride up the outside of a building in a gondola. That is why, especially in the summer, you need to book the gondola rides in advance, otherwise waiting times of several hours are the rule rather than the exception.

Insider Tip

TAKING A BREAK

The American Bar in the Globe – nomen est omen – serves meals from the land of endless opportunities. Its speciality is burgers. (tel: 08 6 00 94 05; Mon–Fri 11am–2pm). Near the Globen is the **Globen Galleria**, a mall with many shops and restaurants.

➕ 181 southwards F3
⊠ Globentorget ▣ Globen

SkyView
☎ 0771 81 10 00; www.globearenas.se/skyview
🕐 Mon–Fri 9:30am–6pm, Sat, Sun 9:30am–4pm
(last gondola 10 min. earlier)
🎟 kr150

INSIDER INFO

The **Sweden Solar System** which stretches over the entire area of Sweden is the world's largest true-to-scale model of our solar system. The Globen represents the sun, the 65cm (25in) size model of the Earth is located in the Swedish Museum of Natural History 6km (4.7mi) away, the Jupiter model, a 7m (23ft) diameter flower bed, at the Stockholm Airport Arlanda 40km (25mi) away – both the distances and the size of the model correspond to the scale measurement 1:20 mill. You can find out where the rest of the planets are at www.swedensolarsystem.se.

🛐 Skogskyrkogården
(Woodland Cemetery)

It is very seldom that a cemetery is selected for the UNESCO list of World Heritage Sites. The Skogskyrkogården, Stockholm's largest cemetery in the Enskede district, is one such exception.

In the reasons UNESCO gave for the cemetery's inclusion during its admission in 1994, it wrote that the Skogskyrkogården was "a prime example…of the fusion of architecture and cultural landscape into a cemetery." It also had a "great influence on the design of graveyards all over the world."

Stockholm's Woodland Cemetery came about as the result of a 1914 international competition, which the two young architects **Gunnar Asplund** and **Sigurd Lewerentz** won with their design. Over the course of more than 25 years, they created Sweden's largest cemetery.

The first building on the huge grounds was the **Skogskapellet (Woodland Chapel)**, which bears a single decoration, the golden sculpture of an angel of death by the well-known sculptor Carl Milles. Another distinctive point is **Meditationslund (Elm Hill)**, which is intended as a place of meditation for those who are in mourning. The two architects apparently took their inspiration for this from the landscape paintings of the German Romantic painter Caspar David Friedrich. The last building erected in the style of Functionalism was the Heliga korsets kapell (Holy Cross Chapel) and the adjoining crematorium. The huge **granite cross** designed by Asplund in 1939, intended not as a religious symbol but instead as a symbol of life's eternal cycle, is located close by. Shortly after completing the work, the architect Gunnar Asplund died. He found his last resting place in the cemetery he designed himself.

At the **Visitors' Centre**, which you reach on foot in about 15 minutes from the main entrance, you can learn more about the history of the cemetery and its architects.

Gunnar Asplund's simple granite cross in the golden light of dusk

TAKING A BREAK
There is also a **café** in the visitors' centre, which serves drinks and simple snacks.

➕ 181 southwards. F3
✉ Sockenvägen 492 (main entrance)
☎ 08 50 83 17 30; www.skogskyrkogarden.se
🕐 Cemetery all year round 24 hr.; Visitors' Centre: May, Sep Sat, Sun 11am–4pm, June–Aug daily 11am–4pm
🚇 Skogskyrkogården
🎟 Free

INSIDER INFO

- There are English **tours** during the summer months (July–Sep Sun 10:30am; kr100). They last about two hours and can be booked online, at the Medeltidsmuseet in Strömparterren Park and – if there are still places available on the day – at the Visitors' Centre.
- Skogskyrkogården is one of the few cemeteries worldwide that has its **own bus line**. Number 183 runs on weekends and public holidays from 10:40am–4:10pm. It sets off every half an hour from the metro station Skogskyrkogården to various stops on the cemetery grounds.

Södermalm

At Your Leisure

52 Mariaberget ("Mary Hill")

Lots of artists live in the old houses along the narrow streets of the Mariaberget district located on the hill of the same name. A dozen galleries line the **Hornsgatspuckeln**, a small street which runs parallel to Hornsgatan. From the **viewing platform** at the end of Monteliusvägen (a path off Bastugatan), you have one of the most beautiful views across Kungsholmen, Stadshus and Gamla Stan. The **Maria Magdalena kyrkan (Maria Magdalena Church)** dates back to 1634, although it received its present look at the end of the 17th/beginning of the 18th century when Nicodemus Tessin the Elder and later his son Nicodemus Tessin the Younger carried out major conversions in the Baroque style. Buried in the church's cemetery is the well-known poet, folk singer and composer Evert Taube (1890–1976). You can find his grave on the right next to the path leading to the church portal.

➕ 181 D2

Insider Tip

Maria Magdalena Kyrkan
➕ 181 E2 ✉ Bellmansgatan 13
☎ 08 4 62 29 60 🚇 Slussen

53 Mosebacke Torg

One of the most beautiful beer gardens in the town is on Mosebacke torg. On the Mosebacke Terrace (➤ 153), you can enjoy a cool drink while looking right out across the city. August Strindberg liked it here and was a regular guest, eventually immortalising Mosebacke in his novel *The Red Room*. A statue of Strindberg by the famous sculptor Carl Eldh reminds people of the connection. The Mosebacke Terrace belongs, like the Mosebacke restaurant (➤ 154), to **Södra Teatern**, Sweden's oldest operating private theatre. The theatre building was inaugurated in 1859, but Mosebacke was already a location where people went to enjoy themselves. The legendary restaurant Stockholm Vapen was here, in which the poet Carl Michael Bellmann was a regular

Insider Tip

Pretty streets and alleys cuddle the Mariaberget

The Rhinish church architecture of the Sofia Church was initially not particularly well received by the Stockholmers

guest. Equally, on Mosebacke torg is the 32m (105ft) high **water tower**, which Ferdinand Boberg built in the National Romantic style in 1896.

✚ 181 F2
☎ 08 53 19 94 90 (ticket office); www.sodrateatern.com
🚇 Slussen

🔢 Sofia kyrkan (Sofia Church)

Perched high up on a 46m (150ft) high hill, the Vita Bergen, overlooking the sea of houses of Södermalm is the Sofia Kyrkan built between

1902 and 1906. The church, which is named after the German wife of King Oscar II, was erected by Gustaf Hermansson. Since he took a lot of his inspiration from the church buildings in Germany, he had to put up with a lot of strong criticism.

A walk through the wooden house district along the **Mäster Pers gränd** and the **Bergsprängargränd** right by the church is well worthwhile. These days, the little red houses are a tourist attraction; in the 19th century, the poorest of the poor lived here. Large families lived in the tiny rooms in cramped conditions, one on top of the other. August Strindberg described their lives in his novel *The Red Room*, which appeared in 1879.

✚ 182 B1 ✉ Borgmästargatan 11
☎ 08 6 15 31 00; www.svenskakyrkan.se/sofia
🕐 Daily 11am–5pm
🚇 Medborgarplatsen

The beer garden on Mosebacke is a popular meeting place for the city dwellers

Where to...
Eat and Drink

Prices
for a main course without drinks
£ under kr200   ££ kr200–kr350   £££ over kr350

There is a mammoth choice of restaurants and bars in the Södermalm district. Although the SoFo district (➤ 136), the area south of Folkungagatan, is the hotspot, night owls will also find many options in other places on Södermalm as well.

And another tip: the new trend in Stockholm is to have a restaurant and bar under one roof. It means guests do not have to go very far when they have finished their meal. However, since our tips in the categories "Eat and Drink" and "Where to... Go Out" do not always offer a clear dividing point, it is well worth looking through both sections before you set off for your evening stroll.

Akkurat ££
A pub at the front, a restaurant at the back, excellent pub food. Steak, burgers, fish and the favourite mussels appear on the menu; to accompany the food, there is alcohol to meet all tastes. The whisky selection is excellent. Sometimes bands perform. At the weekend, unless you have a reservation, it is not normally possible to get a table.
➕ 181 E2
✉ Hornsgatan 18
☎ 08 6 44 00 15; www.akkurat.se
🕐 Mon 11am–midnight, Tue–Fri 11am–1am, Sat 3pm–1am, Sun 6pm–1am
🚇 Slussen

Gondolen £££
Insider Tip Gondolen is a tourist sight and restaurant in one. It lies high up just beneath the Katarina Lift and can thus rightly claim to be the restaurant with the best view of Stockholm. It serves hearty Nordic cuisine. Inexpensive lunch menu. After the meal, you can move into the bar and over beer, wine or cocktails – there are also some very tasty non-alcoholic drinks – continue to lap up the view of the capital.
➕ 181 F2
✉ Stadsgården (entrance via Mosebacke torg or Stadsgården 6, beside Eriks Vinbar)
☎ 08 6 41 70 90; www.eriks.se/gondolen
🕐 Restaurant: Mon–Fri 11:30am–2:30pm and Mon 5pm–11pm, Tue–Fri 5pm–1am, Sat 4pm–1am; Bar: Mon 11:30am–11pm, Tue–Fri 11:30am–1am, Sat 4pm–1am
🚇 Slussen 🚢 Djurgårdsfärjan

Koh Phangan £
When it should be good and really inexpensive, and you are also yearning for Asian aromas, then this local Thai restaurant is a good choice. The setting resembles a beach bar on the eponymous island.
➕ 181 F1
✉ Skånegatan 57
☎ 08 642 50 40; www.kohphangan.se
🕐 Mon–Fri 4pm–1am, Sat noon–1am, Sun noon–midnight
🚇 Medborgarplatsen

Kvarnen ££
The "mill" is a classic beer hall, in which hearty home cooking, such as herring and _köttbullar_ arrive on the table. Södermalm was once a working-class district and the restaurant, when it opened in1909, a place to go for people without much money. The food was simple, but cheap. In the meantime, the

prices have risen, perhaps also due to the fact that Kvarnen has become a bit of a cult place to go. That is thanks to crime author Stieg Larsson, who also used to like eating in the restaurant and had his hero Mikael Blomkvist go there too. The interior is still as it was in the 1920s. Although wine is on the menu, most guests order beer.

🏠 181 F1

✉ Tjärhovsgatan 4

☎ 08 6 43 03 80; www.kvarnen.com

🕐 Mon–Tue 11am–1am, Wed–Fri 11am–3am, Sat noon–3am, Sun noon–1am

Ⓜ Medborgarplatsen

Lasse i Parken £

Pippi Longstocking would come here to eat. The typical Swedish wooden house, painted red, is so cosy inside that you may not wish to leave. Or, at most, out into the garden, which has space for 300 guests. There, sitting under the trees, you can soon leave the stress of city life behind you. During the day, there is an inexpensive lunch menu (11am–2:30pm), coffee and cake, in the evening authentic traditional home cooking and live music. Open from mid-April.

🏠 180 A2

✉ Högalidsgatan 56

☎ 08 6 58 33 95; www.lasseiparken.se

🕐 Mid-April–June, Sep daily 11am–5pm, June–Aug daily 11am–8pm

Ⓜ Hornstull

Linje Tio ££

Tapas bar and restaurant. Decent food and good drinks arrive on the table. Popular with the "cool" people on the block – hence sometimes extremely amusing, on other occasions rather painful. The restaurant is named after tram no. 10, which rolled along Hornsgatan until 1967.

🏠 180 A2

✉ Hornsbruksgatan 24

☎ 08 22 00 21; http://linjetio.com

🕐 Mon–Thu 5pm–1am, Fri 4pm–2am, Sat noon–2am, Sun noon–1am Ⓜ Hornstull

Marie Laveau ££

Café, restaurant and bar under one roof – with its versatility, Marie Laveau caters to the tastes of every night owl. The restaurant operates under the umbrella term of "American Bar" and offers southern states dishes. The restaurant is named after a voodoo priestess – one can only hope that she does not haunt the kitchen. The bar is particularly popular for a drink after the office closes; DJs take over later on. The plainly furnished self-service café (£) serves fast food.

🏠 181 D2

✉ Hornsgatan 66,

☎ 08 6 68 85 00; http://marielaveau.se

🕐 Restaurant: Tue 5pm–10pm, Wed–Sat 5pm–11pm, Sun 1pm–9pm; Bar: Mon, Tue 5pm–11pm, Wed–Sat 5pm–3am, Sun 1pm–9pm; Café Mon–Sat 11am–5pm

Ⓜ Zinkensdamm, Mariatorget

Morfar Ginko ££

"Grandfather Ginko" is a combination of restaurant and bar. In terms of food, you should not expect any miracles. The menu lists trout, steak, sausages, lobster and falafel, an unusual mix that is rather hard to categorise. The bar offers comfortable sofas and excellent drinks – and is one of the most popular places in Södermalm. You can sit outside in the inner courtyard during the summer. By the way, anyone who wants to be cool these days appears to need to have an inhouse hairdresser. Morfar Ginko has kept abreast of that.

🏠 181 E1 ✉ Swedenborgsgatan 13

☎ 08 6 41 13 40; www.morfarginko.se

🕐 Mon–Thu 5pm–1am, Fri 4pm–1am, Sat, Sun noon–1am Ⓜ Mariatorget

Nytorget 6 £–££

At Nytorget 6, the name and address are identical. It receives (not only) the neighbours from 7.30am in the morning for breakfast. At midday and in the evening, it then continues with a modern-international cuisine. How does, for instance, black pudding on cranberry sauce sound? Or an omelette with smoked salmon, spinach and goats' cheese?

➕ 182 B1 ✉ Nytorg 6
☎ 08 6 40 96 55; www.nytorget6.com
🕐 Mon–Tue 7:30am–midnight, Wed–Fri 7:30am–1am, Sat 10am–1am, Sun 10am–midnight
🚇 Medborgarplatsen 🚌 59, 66

Och Himlen Därtill £££

The tax office used to be based in this high-rise. Now a restaurant with a sky bar resides here at over 100m (330ft). When the high-rise was renovated in 2007, another two floors were added. Since then, guests can dine, or nip on a cocktail, with a 360-degree view of Stockholm. The menu offers Nordic cuisine with an international touch. In the evenings, you pay for the view, but the lunch menu at kr135–kr155 is sensationally inexpensive. After the meal, guests can move upstairs to the Skybar for even more view.

Insider Tip

➕ 181 F1 ✉ Götgatan 78
☎ 08 6 60 60 68; www.restauranghimlen.se
🕐 Mon 11:30am–midnight, Tue–Thu 11:30am–1am, Fri 11:30am–3am, Sat noon–3am 🚇 Medborgarplatsen

Östgötakällaren £–££

Anyone in search of a bit of hearty Prussian fare should go to Östgötakällaren. German meals are served in the traditional Södermalm restaurant.

➕ 181 F1 ✉ Östgötagatan 41,
☎ 08 6 43 22 40; www.ostgotakallaren.se
🕐 Mon–Fri 5pm–1am, Sat 3pm–1am, Sun 5pm–1am 🚇 Medborgarplatsen

Pelikan ££

This is where traditional home cooking is offered in the corresponding setting. Anyone looking for a touch of the "old Stockholm" will love it here. Of course, the Pelikan is no longer an insider tip, guests from foreign countries also make their way here on their culinary tours. However, time and again,

Insider Tip

the restaurant and its menu still make a journey back in time an inviting prospect. In the old Pelikan, the predecessor restaurant on the same spot, Sweden's most well-known poet and singer Carl Michael Bellmann (1740–1795) was a regular, hard-drinking guest.

➕ 181 south F1 ✉ Blekingegatan 40
☎ 08 55 60 90 90; www.pelikan.se
🕐 Mon, Tue 4pm–midnight, Wed, Thu 4pm–1am, Fri–Sun noon–1am
🚇 Skanstull

String £

This cosy café is particularly popular with students. They surf here on the internet (free WiFi) while munching on sandwiches or carrot cake. There are also small cooked dishes such as lasagne, and one hot dish is served each day at lunchtime. On Saturdays and Sundays between 9am and 1pm, String rustles up a lavish brunch; costing kr90, for Swedish standards a sensationally low price, so the restaurant regularly bursts at the seams on both mornings. In the summer, there are even a few tables in front of the entrance. The on the whole rather old furnishing is colourfully thrown together – all part of the concept, since you can also buy the furniture.

➕ 182 A1 ✉ Nytorgsgatan 38
☎ 08 7 14 85 14; www.cafestring.com
🕐 Mon–Fri 9am–10pm, Sat, Sun 9am–7pm
🚇 Medborgarplatsen

Where to...
Shop

With its many shops and boutiques, Södermalm is the perfect place for a shopping tour. The choice in SoFo, the area to the south of Folkungagatan, is tremendous. Many art galleries line the Hornsgatspuckeln as well.

CLOTHING/ACCESSORIES/DESIGN

At **Nudie Jeans**, no. 75 Skånegatan (Mon–Fri 11am–6:30pm, Sat 11am–5pm, Sun noon–4pm, metro: Medborgarplatsen), you can buy high-quality fair-trade jeans. Since the proprietors take the sustainability promise seriously, they also offer a free repair service there.

Clothes, accessories, and beautiful things for the home are on offer at the two subsidiaries of **Monki** Götgatan (nos. 19 and 78, Mon–Fri 10am–8pm, Sat 10am–6pm, Sun 11am–5pm/6pm, metro: Slussen).

DesignTorget (Götgatan 31, Mon–Fri 10am–7pm, Sat 10am–6pm, Sun 11am–5:30pm, metro: Slussen) is definitely not a small dealer. The company has shops throughout the north of Europe, six alone of which are in Greater Stockholm; the one in Södermalm is particularly nice. It sells little objects for the house – they are always beautiful and sometimes useful. The range includes everything from the children's' bedroom to the bathroom.

ART & CRAFTS

Located at no. 17 Kocksgatan is **125 Kvadrat** (Mon–Fri 11am–6pm, Sat, Sun 11am–4pm, metro: Folkungagatan), a shop with an adjoining showroom, which it shares with an artists' cooperative. The materials used range from textile to wood and from glass to metal – and all of the artists' work is of the highest quality.

Konsthantverkarna (Mon–Fri 11am–6pm, Sat 11am–4pm, metro: Slussen) at no. 4 Södermalmstorg functions on a similar basis. However, over 100 artists are involved in this cooperative. **Blås & Knåda** (Tue–Fri 11am–6pm, Sat 11am–4pm, Sun noon–4pm, metro: Slussen) at no. 25 Hornsgatan sells glass and ceramic products – every object is handmade and unique.

SECOND-HAND

Second-hand brand clothing, occasionally unique pieces, fill the racks at **Judits Second Hand** at no. 75 Hornsgata (Mon–Fri 11am–6pm, Sat 11am–4:30pm, metro: Zinkensdamm).

Awaiting you just a few paces farther on is the second-hand shop of designer label **Filippa K** (Hornsgata 77, Mon–Fri 11am–6pm, Sat 11am–4pm, metro: Zinkensdamm). Besides the "usual" second-hand products, this shop also receives the sample design pieces from the Fillippa K collection; occasionally, men, too, have a good chance of finding an original piece.

Lisa Larsson sells stock on return in her secondhand shop at no. 48 Bondegatan 48 (Tue–Fri 1pm–6pm, Sat 11am–3pm metro: Medborgarplatsen). She specialises in clothing from the 1930s to 1970s.

Beyond Retro, London's leading shop for vintage clothing has a branch in Södermalm (Brännkyrkagatan 82, Mon–Fri 11am–7pm, Sat 11am–5pm, Sun noon–4pm, metro: Zinkensdamm).

Where to...
Go Out

Many Stockholmers combine an evening meal with a visit to a bar. Or they head for a less expensive bar or drink a glass of wine at home before they set off. The result: Stockholm's party life generally doesn't really get going until late in the evening.

That applies for the whole town, but especially for the main party

Södermalm

districts. Those who arrive early thus save themselves long queues at the entrance and profit from the reduced entrance fee. Those over 18 who have attained their majority should not be under any illusion that they will get into all the clubs though. The age limit is often 20 or even 23. Young and young-looking adults should be prepared to be asked their age at the entrance and take identity papers with them.

Debaser Medis
Live music several times a week. In the restaurant, you can build up your strength for the concert and then also benefit from the fact that you have priority entry.
➕ 181 F1 ✉ Medborgarplatsen 8
☎ 08 6 94 79 00; http://debaser.se
🕐 depending on the event
🚇 Medborgarplatsen

Mosebacke
In addition to the **Södra Teatern** on Mosebacke, in which excellent theatre performances take place, there are also a whole range of locations in which you can eat, drink and party. The **Mosebacketerrassen** beer garden next to the theatre is, owing to the view alone, the most beautiful in the city. With a cold drink in your hand, you can look out over Stockholm. It serves light meals as well.

The **Mosebacke Etablissement** restaurant mainly has vegetarian dishes on its menu, but meat and fish can be ordered to go with them.

The view from the **Södra Bar** is as good as the one from the beer garden, the drinks are a little more refined. The bar over the theatre is a retreat for all those who would like to end the evening in a relaxed setting. From time to time, live music heightens the enjoyment of the view and cocktails.
➕ 181 F2 ✉ Mosebacke torg 1am–3
🚇 Slussen

Södra Teatern
☎ 08 53 19 94 90 (ticket office); www.sodrateatern.com

Mosebacketerrassen
🕐 Summer Mon–Thu 11am–10pm, Fri, Sat until 11pm

Mosebacke Etablissement
☎ 08 53 19 93 79 🕐 lunch Mon–Fri 11am–2pm, dinner Tue 5pm–10pm, Wed, Thu 5pm–1am, Fri, Sat 5pm–2am (kitchen closes at 10pm), Brunch Sun 11am–4pm

Södra Bar
☎ 08 53 19 94 90 🕐 Fri, Sat 5pm–2am

Patricia
Aboard this old English warship are several bars – inside and on deck – a restaurant and at the weekends from 11pm also a nightclub (Sun Gay Club). It is hard to believe that this party ship was not only involved in the evacuation from Dunkirk but also in the invasion in Normandy. After the war, the *Patricia* was one of the escort vessels for the royal yacht and, in this capacity, lay at anchor off Helsinki in 1952 when Queen Elizabeth II visited the Summer Olympics. Since 1986, the ship has had been at its final mooring in Stockholm. And people have been partying there ever since.
➕ 180 C2 ✉ Söder Mälarstrand, Kajplats 19,
☎ 08 7 43 05 70; www.patricia.st
🕐 Wed, Thu 5pm–midnight, Fri–Sun 6pm–5am (Nightclub from 11pm)
🚇 Slussen 🚌 85 Kungsholmen

Side Track
One of the oldest gay bars in Stockholm. In the small restaurant at the front you can order very satisfactory Nordic cuisine with an international touch (also vegetarian and vegan) for reasonable prices. Behind the bar it is somewhat cosier. Very friendly service
➕ 181 D2 ✉ Wollmar Yxkullsgatan 7
☎ 08 6 41 16 88; www.sidetrack.nu
🕐 Wed–Sat 6pm–1am, food until 11pm
🚇 Mariatorget.

Excursions

Millesgården

Carl Milles (1875–1955) was Sweden's most important 20th century sculptor, and was also well-known internationally. In 1906 he purchased together with his wife, the Austrian portrait painter Olga Granner, a piece of land on the island of Lidingö and had an elegant house built. His residence, adorned with many sculptures, is now a museum.

Initially the couple lived in their home in the north-east of Stockholm until 1931, followed by an almost 20-year stay in the USA, where Milles worked at the Cranbook Academy of Art near Detroit (which is where you will find the largest collection of his sculptures outside Millesgården). After their return, the two artists turned their home into a sculpture garden. This also involved setting up **replicas** of Milles' monumental sculptures and fountains, which are located in other parts of Sweden and the USA.

When Carl Milles died in 1955, he was buried in the **chapel** in the park. Since 1999, there has been an **art gallery** on the property, in which temporary exhibitions of Swedish and international artists regularly take place.

The Sculpture Garden

The garden laid out in terraces, which was also extended after the death of Carl Milles encompasses around 1.8ha (4.5 acres). Thanks to its location on an elevation, Milles'

GOD, THE FATHER ON HEAVEN'S ARCH

Perhaps Milles' most spectacular work was not fully completed until 40 years after his death. It is not in Millesgården, but in **Nacka Strand Harbour** on the way into Stockholm. Back in 1946, Milles completed a preliminary design in bronze entitled *The Rainbow. Lord placing new stars on heaven*; the plan was to put the original in front of the UNO building in New York. Yet the idea was never put into effect. After the bronze piece, which was kept in Millesgården, it was eventually the American sculptor Marshall M. Fredericks – who had worked closed with Milles for many years – who completed the artwork. The imposing sculpture shows God as he is seated on an around 18m (59ft) high, water-spouting, parabolic-shaped arch. The arch symbolises the firmament. Standing at its base is an angel to whom God is handing stars to place in the night sky.

works compete with the wonderful view of Stockholm and the skerries. Typical for the artistic creativity of the famous Swedish sculptor are the figures standing high on a column or pedestal as well as the fountain adorned with one or more figures.

Millesgården encompasses the upper, central and lower terraces, the studio garden and the terrace for his wife Olga. Included among some of the most well-known works here are: *Lilla Tritonen* (*Little Triton*, the original is in the park Waldemarsudde, ▶ 115), the *Bågskytten* (*the Archer*, in front of the Liljevalchs art gallery, ▶ 128), *Vingarna*, (*The Wings*, Skeppsholmen Bridge), the Gustav-Wasa statue (Nordic Museum, ▶ 119), the *Orfeus Group* (Konserthuset, ▶ 57) and the *Poseidon Fountain* (Götaplatsen in Gothenburg).

The original of the 1930 *Poseidon Fountain* stands on the Götaplatsen in Gothenburg, the replica on the lower terrace of Millesgården

✉ Herserudsvägen 32, Lidingö
☎ 08 4 46 75 90; www.millesgarden.se
🕐 May–Sep daily 11am–5pm, Oct–April Tue–Sun 11am–5pm
🚇 Ropsten, then Bus 201, 202, 204, 205, 206, 211, 212 or 221, followed by a 7 min. walk
💷 kr150

Excursions

Drottningholms Slott
(Drottningholm Palace)

Of all the 17th-century royal palaces in Sweden, Drottningholm has to be among the best preserved. Together with the park, the palace theatres and the Chinese pavilion, it offers a unique ensemble, and has been a UNESCO national heritage site since 1991.

The royal palace is situated just a few kilometres outside Stockholm on **Lovön Island** in Lake Mälar. Although you can also reach it with the bus or car, the nicest trip is with one of the **steamboats**, which regularly leave from the quay at Stadshuset (▶ 50). In 1981, the royal family moved from the City Palace to Drottningholm and since then have resided in the south section of the building. However, the majority of the palace and park complex is open to the public all year round.

Insider Tip

The Palace

There was already a much smaller palace of the same name on Lovön in the 16th century. After a fire had destroyed its predecessor, the widowed Queen Hedvig Eleonora commissioned Nicodemus Tessin, the Elder to build a new palace. After his death in 1681, his son continued his work and was able to complete it in 1701.

The original Baroque interior dates back to the 17th century. One of the special highlights is the **Ehrenstrahl Room**, with paintings by David Klöcker Ehrenstrahl, Sweden's most important Baroque artist, the **staircase** with its battle paintings, sculptures and portraits as well as the magnificent **bedroom of Hedvig Eleonora**.

People call the Drottningholm Palace the "Versailles of the North"

Princess Luise Ulrike of Prussia succeeded Hedvig Eleonora, who received Drottningholm Palace on the occasion of her marriage to the Crown Prince of Sweden, Adolf Fredrik of Holstein-Gottorf (1711–1771), as a dowry. She had some of the palace decorated in the Rococo style, a particularly beautiful example from her time is the **Library**.

The Palace Park

The oldest part of the palace garden was laid out by Hedvig Eleonora as a **Baroque Garden**. Its focal point is the **Hercules Fountain** with bronze figures by the sculptor Adriaen de Vries. He created all the other bronze works in the park as well. When Gustav III took over Drottningholm in 1777, he had a modern **English landscape park** laid out to the north of the Baroque garden. In the 19th century, the Baroque garden fell into decay, and it was not until the 1950s and 1960s that it was restored under King Gustav VI Adolf.

The Palace Theatre

Constructed in 1766, the Palace Theatre still has the original furnishings, which include interior décor from the Gründerzeit (Founders' Period). It is the only Rococo theatre in Europe, in which the original stage machinery still works and in which all the original sets have been retained. Opera performances take place here in summer at which the orchestra plays historical instruments.

Insider Tip

Chinese Pavilion

The little pavilion in the south part of the rambling park was a birthday present for Luise Ulrike of Prussia. The wooden structure was replaced by a sturdier building in the 1760s. It contains one of the most spectacular Rococo interiors with Chinoiserie in Europe. The **Yellow Room** with its varnished Chinese panels is a real eye catcher.

✉ Drottningholm, Ekerö, Lovön Island
☎ 08 4 02 62 80; www.kungahuset.se
🕐 May–Sep daily 10am–4:30pm, April daily 11am–3:30pm, Oct Fri–Sun 11am–3:30pm, Nov–March Sat, Sun noon–3pm G176, 177, 301–323
🚢 Strömma Kanalbolaget from Stadshusbron; www.strommakanalbolaget.com
✋ kr120. Combined ticket with pavilion: kr180

INSIDER INFO

- If you wish, you can take part in one of the informative **tours** through the palace, which are also available in English (June–Sep daily 10am, noon, 2pm and 4pm, Oct–May Sat, Sun noon and 4pm). From May–September, the tickets cost kr30, the rest of the year, the tours are included in the entrance fee.
- You can buy the **tickets** to Drottningholm Palace online. The site does not provide any discounts.

Artipelag

The unique natural setting of Stockholm's skerries combined with a first-class art and culture project: that neatly describes the new Artipelag art centre, which opened on Hålludden near Stockholm in 2012.

Artipelag is a made-up name using the words "art", "activities" and "archipelago". The around 10,000m² (110,000ft²) of the building include the art hall, a concert and event hall, a conference area, several restaurants and a design shop; a hotel is also planned. It is not only the building itself, but the skerries around 20km (12.5mi) east of the Swedish capital that are so impressive.

Initiator and financer of the project is Björn Jakobson, founder of the Swedish company BabyBjörn. In the art hall, it is not only the art objects from the family collection that are on view; Artipelag is also intended to host top-class **temporary exhibitions** from the most varied of genres – from classic and modern art to architecture and design and crafts.

You can reach the art centre via land routes, or – which is much nicer – with the excursion ship from Stockholm (the journey lasts about an hour). The gallery is almost hidden from the water. The building construction which is impregnated with creosote blends in well with the superb setting. Across the Baggensfjärden, you can see the Saltsjöbaden and the island of Älgö in the distance. Anyone wanting to have a bit of exercise can wander along **nature paths** through the woods or follow the wooden board-walks along the water's edge. You should not miss the view from the **roof terrace** over the bay and the skerry garden.

Art and nature enter a successful symbiosis in the Artipelag art centre

Insider Tip

✉ Artipelagstigen 1, Gustavsberg
☎ 08 57 01 30 00; www.artipelag.se
🕐 July–Aug daily 11am–5pm, except for Mondays
🚇 Slussen, then with bus 474 to the Gustavsbergs centrum stop and on with bus 468 to the Hålludden stopy
⛴ from Stockholm-Nybrokajen, Jetty no. 8
💰 kr150

Walks & Tours

Walks & Tours

1 ON THE TRAIL OF STIEG LARSSON
Walk

LENGTH: 3km (2mi) **DURATION:** 1.5 hours
START: Bellmangata (Slussen) ✚ 181 E1
END: Mosebacketorg (Slussen) ✚ 181 E/F1

Stieg Larsson's thriller the Millennium Trilogy, which was published in Britain under the titles of: *The Girl with the Dragon Tattoo*, *The Girl Who Played with Fire* and *The Girl Who Kicked the Hornet's Nest* ranks among the most successful books of this century. Stieg Larsson did not experience this success, because he died in November 2004 just before the publication of the first volume. Visitors to Stockholm can take part in a tour organised by the City Museum (➤ 140) to some of the settings in the book. Those who wish to do their own investigations can pick up a map provided by the tourist information office in Kulturhuset (➤ 35) and follow the trail on their own. One possible route is outlined below.

❶–❷

Mikael Blomkvist, the journalist and main character in Larsson's books lived in **Bellmansgatan (no. 1)** the Mariaberget district. In real life, Blomkvist would have remained shut up in his house forever. Unlike the portrayal in the novel, there is actually no entrance on to Bellmansgatan. The "real" in-habitants leave it on the Bastugatan side. For the Swedish film version

of the book, Blomkvist's home was moved about 50m (165ft) further up the street. There actually is a man called Mr Blomquist living in the first house in Bellmansgatan, who claims in a convincing fashion that he has never read the *Millennium* thrillers.

At the end of the Bastugatan, you reach **Lundabron** and the house in which Larsson's second main character, computer hacker Lisbeth Salander, grew up.

❷–❸

Just a few paces from there at 78 Hornsgatan is the **Mellqvist coffee bar**, one of Blomkvist's favourite cafés. Stieg Larsson also used to enjoy drinking his coffee here. The same applies for **Café Java** at 29A Hornsgatan, although there is a new owner here in the meantime and the café is now called **For Friends** (in the Hollywood production, the coffeehouse scenes were not filmed in either one of the cafés).

❸–❹

Just past the Maria Magdalena kyrkan you reach the corner of the **Götgatan/Hökens Gata** and the editorial rooms of the *Millennium* magazine of which Blomkvist is the boss. The building at least was used for the exterior shots in the film. The interior shots were record-ed in the old state archive on Birger Jarls torg (2a) on Riddarholmen.

Bellmansgatan 1 – this is where Blomkvist lives

Kvarnen, the regular haunt of Blomkvist and Salander

lover Miriam Wu takes place here. The next stop Fiskargatan 9, can be reached via Östgötagatan. This is where Lisbeth Salander lives in a noble penthouse with a view over Stockholm. Her name does not appear on the door, only "V. Kulla" – for Swedes a clear reference to the Villekulla Villa, the name of Pippi Longstocking's home. Like Pippi, Lisbeth is also a girl who rebels against the establishment in her own special way.

If you want to celebrate your wedding on the original site, just go ahead: you can rent the rooms in the stylish building.

In the book, *Millennium* anyway has its office in **Götgatan (no. 19)**, which is where Greenpeace is also based. At the time of the film production, however, the building was surrounded by scaffolding, so that it was necessary to do the recordings a few metres further along. The **Seven-Elven shop**, in which Lisbeth Salander does all her shopping is also in Götgatan (no. 25).

4–5

By Medborgarplatsen, you turn off into Tjärhovsgatan. That is where you will find the **Kvarnen** restaurant (no. 4; ➤ 150), in which both Blomkvist and Lisbeth Salander often used to eat. Even the famous scene in which Salander kisses her

5–6

The walk ends in the beer garden by the **Södra Teatern** (➤ 153) at Mosebacketorg. This is where Larsson often used to eat and drink a glass of beer. And this is where the wake was held after Larsson's funeral.

TAKING A BREAK

Plenty of restaurants around Medborgarplatsen ensure that you will not go hungry. Those wishing to eat in an original *Millennium* setting can go to Kvarnen (➤ 150).

Insider Tip

Walks & Tours

2 THROUGH DJURGÅRDEN
Cycling Tour

LENGTH: 13km (8mi) **DURATION:** 4–8 hours, depending on the number and duration of the museum visits
START/END: Djurgårdsbron (76) 182 C4

This bicycle tour, which you can naturally do on foot, takes you from Djurgårdsbron to the most important sights on the green museum island. Relatively little car traffic, a lot of green space and a lot of space for a break by the water make this excursion a real joy.

1–2
Those who do not have their own bikes with them can hire them in Sjöcaféet (► 130) on Djurgårdsbron. From here, cycle just a few hundred metres south and you will be standing at the entrance of the **Nordic Museum** (► 119). Before you go in, look at the museum building that resembles a castle with its numerous turrets.

2–3
It is hardly worth getting back on your bike to move on to the **Vasa Museum** (► 104), which is on Galärvarvsvägen. Awaiting you in

the museum is the *Vasa*, the proud battleship of King Gustav II, which in actual fact had anything but a proud demise.

3–4
After the visit to the Vasa Museum, it is worth taking a look at the ships in the museum harbour, before continuing your trip on the nearby Djurgårdsvägen. Once past the Liljevalch's Art Gallery (► 128), you can visit **ABBA The Museum** (► 112).

4–5
Another short trip along the Djurgårdsvägen, and you will be standing in front of the entrance to the **Skansen** Open-Air Museum (► 109), in which typical farmsteads, houses and other buildings

164

from Sweden's rich history have been gathered together.

5–6

Then you continue on Djurgårdsvägen, which becomes Ryssviksvägen at Wasahamnen yacht harbour. Afterwards, turn right onto Prince Eugens väg and go through the park to **Waldemarsudde** (► 115). This is where Prince Eugen pursued his passions for painting and landscape gardening; he left posterity a residence with lots of artworks in a dream location.

TAKING A BREAK

There are lots of benches along the way that present a perfect invitation for a picnic by the water or on the grass. There is no shortage of cafés either. **Café Blockhusporten** (► 125) is on the eastern tip of the island, directly by the water with a view of a busy shipping route. Near Rosendal Palace is **Rosendals Trädgård** (► 130), renowned for its delicious homemade cakes. And just before you reach the tour's goal, the final distraction is the enchanting garden café **Villa Godthem** (► 120).

extensive art collection, which is now open to the public.

7–8

A couple of turns of the wheel and you are the most eastern point of Djurgården Island; turn left here and continue riding along the water to the starting point. On the way, there is another enticing little detour possible to Rosendal Palace (► 129), which was built in the Empire style for King Karl XIV Johan.

6–7

Cycle on mainly by the water to the **Thiel Gallery** (► 124). The rich banker Ernest Thiel had a dream villa built for himself in the middle of the woods and put together an

8–1

Continue through Lusthusportens park. When you reach the blue gate with gold adornments, it is not much farther to Djurgårdsbron.

By the Djurgårdsbrunn canal – green idyll in the city centre

3 THE UNKNOWN SÖDERMALM
Walk

LENGTH: 7km (4.5mi) **DURATION:** 2 hr., longer depending on length of time spent swimming or having a picnic
START/END: Katarinahissen (🚇 Slussen) ✚ 181 F2

From the viewing platform on Monteliusvägen, you look out over the Old Town, which is dominated by the tower of the Riddarholmen Church

Södermalm was once the working-class district in the town, the area where the poor and marginalised of Stockholm society used to live – labourers and the unemployed, prostitutes and thieves. The city's bourgeoisie rarely ventured there – and if they did it was usually because they were going to the Södra Teatern and the beer garden next door. From there, they could look out over "their" Stockholm, aloof from violent crime and organised criminality. It is an image that Södermalm has long put to one side; the district has been "hip" for around the last ten years: Anyone who lives here is no longer pitied but envied. This city walk leads through the western, less well-known, and green part of the district.

🕧-🕜

Some of the main sights are near the busy Slussen traffic junction, which is only a few minutes' walk from the southern end of Gamla Stan; furthermore the Green Line of the Tunnelbana stops here. Until recently, you could still take the **Katarinahissen** (► 140), an old lift from 1883, up to the Södermalm hills. In the meantime, however, it has been closed down and thus this unusual form of transport is denied you. The vista from its viewing platform, which is still open to the public, provides a stylish introduction to the tour. Should you later wish to leave out the detour to the observation platform on Monteliusvägen, you should definitely not miss the **view down on Gamla Stan**. Just around the corner on the Ryssgården is the **City Museum** (▶ 140). Like many of the buildings in the town, it was built by the Stralsund-born architect Nicodemus Tessin the Older (1615–81). The museum offers guided city tours. You can also book walks on special topics, like the ABBA tour.

using plans by Nicodemus Tessin the Older.

In **Brännkyrkagatan**, just a short way away from the church, 19th century women used to practise the oldest profession, a career choice that is now forbidden in modern Sweden. Via Bastugatan and Monteliusvägen (▶ 148), you

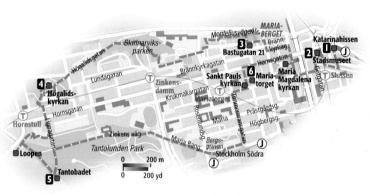

🄻–🄱

Go past the **Maria Magdalena kyrkan** (▶ 148) from 1659 at the far eastern end of Hornsgatan and you will come to the Mariaberget district. The church was also built

come to one of the most beautiful viewing places in the city. Great admirers of Swedish literature can make a short stop at the former home of famous writer **Ivar Lo-Johansson** in Bastugatan (21),

A popular meeting place in summer: Tantolunden Park

Walks & Tours

in which there is also a museum (Mon–Fri 11am–3pm).

🔢3–4

Through **Skinnarviksparken** – with its many, many beautiful viewing points – you reach Högalidsgatan, which leads up to the church of the same name. The **Högalidskyrkan** (Mon–Fri 11am–6pm, Sat 11am–4pm, Sun 10am–4pm) was built in the National Romantic style between 1916 and 1923 using plans by Ivar Tengbom. Another work by Tengbom is of course the Stockholm Concert Hall, in which the Nobel Prizes are presented each year.

🔢4–5

After a flying visit to the church, you cross the large Hornsgatan, go past ugly apartment building, down Lingnagatan and on a few metres to Tantolunden Park, the popular recreation area of the "Södermalmers" in summer. There you can reach – in view of Liljeholmsbron – the cool beach bar **Loopen** (Hornstull strand 6). For those who want to splash around in the water as opposed to just looking at it, 🚻 **Tantobadet** offers the perfect opportunity.

ROYAL SILK   Insider Tip

At the end – or at the beginning – of the walk, it is well worth making a detour to **K. A. Almgrens, a silk-weaving company**, which is not far from Maria Magdalena kyrkan at no. 15A Repslagargatan. The weaving machines there are almost 100 years old, and, despite that, are still working. The family company, which produced the finest silk for the crown family and affluent merchants is the only silk-weaving company that has been preserved north of the Alps. There are spectacular silk materials on sale at the museum shop (tel: 08 6 40 19 01; www.kasiden.se, Mon–Fri 10am–4pm, Sat, Sun 11am–3pm).

🔢5–6

You leave Tantolunden on Zinkens väg and follow Maria Bangata to **Bergsgruvan** – a kind of mini mountain in the middle of Södermalm. When you walk up Timmermansgatan, you pass St. Pauls kyrka to reach **Mariatorget**. Here it is worth taking a small break to sit on one of the benches on the square. This will enable you to take a good look at all the statues set up here, including one of the mystic Emanuel Swedenborg; the sculpture in the central fountain depicts the battle of the Nordic God Thor with the sea serpent Jörmungandr. It is actually also quite fascinating to watch the people who meet here on one of the district's main squares.

🔢6–1

Walking along Hornsgatan, you reach the starting point of this walk after a few hundred metres. Or you can tramp on to the nearby SoFo district (► 136) and spend the end of the day wandering round the shops or enjoying a drink.

The sculpture *Tors fiske* ("Thor's fishing") forms the centrepiece of Mariatorget

Practicalities

Practicalities

BEFORE YOU GO

WHAT YOU NEED

● Required
○ Suggested
▲ Not required

Some countries require a passport to remain valid for a minimum period (usually at least six months) beyond the date of entry – check beforehand.

	UK	USA	Canada	Australia	Ireland	Netherlands
Passport	●	●	●	●	●	●
Visa	▲	▲	▲	▲	▲	▲
Onward or Return Ticket	▲	▲	▲	▲	▲	▲
Health Inoculations	▲	▲	▲	▲	▲	▲
Health Documentation (➤ 174, Health)	○	○	○	○	○	○
Travel Insurance	○	○	○	○	○	○
Driver's Licence (national)	●	●	●	●	●	●
Car Insurance Certificate (if using own car)	○	n/a	n/a	n/a	○	○
Car Registration Document (if using own car)	●	n/a	n/a	n/a	●	●

WHEN TO GO

High season — Low season

JAN	FEB	MAR	APRIL	MAY	JUNE	JULY	AUG	SEP	OCT	NOV	DEC
Low season	Low season	Low season	Low season	Low season	High season	High season	High season	Low season	Low season	Low season	Low season
-1°C	-1°C	3°C	8°C	14°C	19°C	22°C	20°C	15°C	9°C	5°C	2°C
30°F	30°F	37°F	46°F	57°F	66°F	72°F	68°F	59°F	48°F	41°F	36°F
Sunshine and showers	Sunshine and showers	Sunshine and showers	Sun	Sun	Sun	Sunshine and showers	Sunshine and showers	Sunshine and showers	Sunshine and showers	Sunshine and showers	Sunshine and showers

Sun — Sunshine and showers

The diagram shows the **highest average daily temperature** for the respective month. Essentially, you can visit Stockholm all year round, but the **summer months** of June, July and August are naturally the nicest. T-shirt weather is guaranteed thanks to the stable good weather periods, which are not that seldom, and up to 18½ hours of sun a day. The town is relatively empty during the summer holidays when the Stockholmers set off for the countryside. Hotels in which otherwise there are normally a lot of bookings from business guests encourage alternative guests with special offers. In the **winter months**, the short days in particular are not everyone's cup of tea.

GETTING ADVANCE INFORMATION

Websites

- **www.visitstockholm.com**
- **www.visitsweden.com**

Practicalities

GETTING THERE

By Air The international airports serving Stockholm are Arlanda (www.arlanda.se) and Skavsta (www.skavsta.se) near Nykopping. They are 40 and 100km (25 and 60mi) respectively from the city centre.

From the UK British Airways (www.british airways.com), SAS (www.flysas.com), Norwegian Air (www.norwegian.com) and Monarch (www.monarch.co.uk) offer non-stop scheduled flights to Stockholm from London, Manchester, Birmingham, Edinburgh and Bristol. Budget carriers such as Ryanair (www.ryanair.com) usually arrive in Skavsta. KLM (www.klm.com) though some of these flights require transfers.

From the United States and Canada United (www.united.com) Lufthansa (www.lufthansa.com) as well as SAS and Norwegian Air offer non-stop scheduled flights to Stockholm from the main hubs of New York City, Chicago, Los Angeles, Oakland and Fort Lauderdale. Manchester, Birmingham, Edinburgh and Bristol. The main hubs for flights from Canada are Toronto, Montreal, Vancouver, Calgary and Edmonton with airlines such as Air Canada (www.aircanada.com) and United.

By Car If you decide to take the car to Stockholm, a good option is to leave from Dover or Folkestone on the ferry, drive to Puttgarden (Germany), catch a ferry from Puttgarden to Rødby (Denmark), drive to Hensingor and then catch a ferry to Helsingborg in Sweden. You are then just 555km (344 mi) from Stockholm. (https://www.freightlink.co.uk/knowledge/how-do-i/uk-sweden). In Stockholm, a **toll** (kr10–20) is paid when entering and leaving the city, and these are charged to your credit card if you have a hire car. In Sweden, drivers must use dipped headlights during the day as well. Winter tyres are compulsory between 1 December and 31 March. The alcohol limit is 0.2.

TIME

Sweden lies within the **Central European time** zone (CET), i.e. one hour ahead of **Greenwich Mean Time** (GMT). Clocks are adjusted forwards one hour for **summer time** in March (GMT+1). They're put back again in October.

CURRENCY & FOREIGN EXCHANGE

The **national currency** is the Swedish krona (SEK); the notes in circulation are kr20, kr50, kr100, kr500 and kr1,000 and the coins are kr1, kr2, kr5 and kr10.

Currency Exchange Stockholm Airport has exchange offices (daily 8am–9pm). You can also change money in many post offices.

Debit and Credit Cards: Swedes often pay even very small amounts with their credit cards; all well-known credit cards are accepted.

ATMs: There ATMS everywhere in the town (Swedish: *bankomat*), where holidaymakers can withdraw cash. Beware! The charges for withdrawing cash with EC cards are quite high.

Reporting Lost Cards: American Express: 07 71 29 56 00; Diners Club 08 14 68 78; Eurocard 08 14 6878; Mastercard, tel. 020 79 13 24; Visa Global Card Assistance Service, tel: 020 79 56 75.

TOURIST INFORMATION OFFICES

Stockholm Visitor Center
Kulturhuset
Sergels torg 5
10327 Stockholm
☎ 08 5 08 28 508

Arlanda Visitor Center
Arlanda Airport Terminal 2 and5
hours daily, staffed 6am–midnight | arrival hall,
terminal 5 | tel. 08 7 97 60 00

Practicalities

NATIONAL HOLIDAYS

1 January	New Year's Day
6 January	Epiphany
March/April	Good Friday, Easter Monday
1 May	Labour Day
May/June	Ascension Day
6 June	National Holiday
Weekend between 19 & 25 June	Midsummer
1st Sat in November	All Saints' Day
24–26 December	Christmas Eve, Christmas
31 December	New Year's Eve

ELECTRICITY

 The power supply in Sweden is 220 volts. Travellers from outside continental Europe should use an adaptor.

OPENING HOURS

○ Shops
● Offices
● Banks
● Museums/Monuments
● Pharmacies

8am 9am 10am noon 1pm 2pm 5pm 6pm 7pm

☐ Day   ☐ Midday   ☐ Evening

Generally *systembolaget* (off-licences) are open Mon–Fri 9am–6pm and Sat until 1pm, 2pm or 4pm. You can shop in some **department stores** until 8pm, 10pm, Sundays noon–4pm. A lot of **grocery stores** are also open late. There are no standard times for the **tourist sights**; the opening and closing times vary considerably.

CONCESSIONS

The Stockholm Card was discontinued at the turn of the year 2015/16. **However, 17 state museums** now offer visitors free admission. In Stockholm these are: Army Museum, Hallwyl Collection, Swedish History Museum, Royal Coin Cabinet, The Royal Armoury, Mediterranean Museum, Moderna Museum, Museum of Ethnography, National Centre for Architecture and Design, National Museum, The Museum for Eastern Antiquities, The National Maritime Museum.

TIPS/GRATUITIES

Tipping is not as prevalent in Sweden as it is in England and the USA. **At the restaurant** in the evening or in the **taxi**, just round up the sum or add a little tip if you were happy with the service.

TIME DIFFERENCES

Stockholm (CET)
12 noon

←
London (GMT)
11am

→
New York (EST)
6am

→
Los Angeles (PST)
3am

→
Sydney (AEST)
9pm

STAYING IN TOUCH

Post: There are no separate post offices in Sweden anymore; stamps are for sale at petrol stations, in supermarkets and at kiosks (Pressbyrån). The blue post boxes are only for regional post, the national and international post has to be put in the yellow post boxes.

Public telephones: The code for Stockholm is 08, for conversations from abroad leave the 0 off. Public telephones are rare these days. You can buy telephone cards at petrol stations, in supermarkets and at kiosks, and it is also possible to pay for phone calls using the usual credit cards. Telephone numbers with the 020 prefix are for connections that are free of charge.

International Dialling Codes:
United Kingdom: 0044; Republic of Ireland: 00353; USA/Canada: 001; Australia: 0061; Sweden 0046

Mobile phones *(mobil):* Almost everyone in Sweden possesses a mobile phone. In some cases it can be cheaper to use a prepaid card from a Swedish provider like Telia (www.telia.se) or (www.comviq.se)

WiFi and Internet: Internet cafés in the old sense have almost died out, but most hotels provide their guests with free internet access via the hotel's own computer or WLAN. In many cafés and in the Stockholm Visitor Center you can surf free of charge. What is very useful in this connection is the "WiFi Map" app, with which you can find many public WLAN hotspots in Stockholm. Some of them are open lines, other require a password.

PERSONAL SAFETY

Stockholm is regarded as a very safe town. However, it the very busy areas and in jostling crowds the normal precautions should be taken:

- There are pickpockets in Sweden, as there are in every big city. Thus avoid taking more money and valuables with you than are absolutely necessary, and leave your important papers in the hotel safe!
- Since thieves also break into cars, you should not leave any valuables in the car.
- The Foreign Office advices strongly against picking up strangers. This could result in criminal prosecution for migrant smuggling.

Police Assistance:
☎ 112 from any phone

POLICE	112
FIRE	112
AMBULANCE	112

Practicalities

HEALTH

 Insurance: If you present the European health insurance document (EHIC),40 you will have your costs refunded when you return home. Recommendation: take out a personal health insurance for travel abroad that also includes the costs for return transport.

 Medical Emergencies (including the dentist): City Akuten, Apelsbergsgatan 48; tel: 020 15 01 50; www.cityakuten.se.

 Weather: In Nordic countries, not in small part due to the fact that the sun shines much longer in the summer, there is also the risk of sunburn. So, don't forget to take along some sun cream and a hat.

 Drugs: Chemists are open during the normal working hours. Apoteket C W Scheele at no. 64 Klarabergsgatan (Metro T-Centralen) is open 24/7.

 Safe Water: The drinking water is of a very good quality.

CUSTOMS

EU citizens may import **alcohol and tobacco** for their own personal use tax-free, and the allowance is very generous (90l wine, 110l beer, 10l hard liquor). For **non-EU citizens** the permitted quantities are much lower: 1l spirits over 22 vol.-% or 2l under 22 vol.-% or 2l sparkling wine and 2l wine. Only non-EU citizens can claim back part of the **VAT** when they leave the country. Information: www.globalblue.com.

TRAVELLING WITH A DISABILITY

Almost all public institutions such as hotels, restaurants, supermarket and urban transport are well-equipped for people with disabilities. Detailed information is available from: De Handikappades Riksförbund; tel: 08 6 85 80 00; http://dhr.se.

CHILDREN

Museums offer free admission and often special exhibitions for children and adolescents. Special attractions for children are marked out in this book with the logo shown above.

TOILETS

Public toilets (that charge between kr5–kr10) can be found in all the big department stores. The website www.toalett.nu and the free app "Toahjälpen" (available only for iPhone) help you find other options, too.

SMOKING

It is even harder for smokers in Sweden than it is in England. Smoking is prohibited almost everywhere.

EMBASSIES & CONSULATES

UK
☎ 08 671 30 00

USA
☎ 08 783 53 00

Ireland
☎ 08 550 40 40

Australia
☎ 08 613 29 00

Canada
☎ 08 453 30 00

Useful Words and Phrases

Swedish belongs to the North Germanic, Scandinavian language group. A characteristic linguistic feature of the language is that the **definite article** is expressed as a word suffix (e.g. vägen = the path (masculine noun), kyrkan = the church (feminine noun)). This can lead to confusion in translation: "Stortorget" stands on the signposts of many towns and means "The Market Square".

It may avoid some despair as you flick through a Swedish telephone book or dictionary if you are aware of the fact that Å, Ä and Ö follow Z in the **Swedish alphabet**.

The following list includes some of the letters that differ from the English pronunciation:

g appears hard as in "gun", but is never soft as in 'gem' (see below).
r sounds like a Spanish r; when followed by d, l, or t, it is not pronounced
s is always pronounced as in "sell", never with the z sound as in 'was'.
c is like the s in "sit" when followed by e, i, y. Otherwise pronounced as k.
g is pronounced as y when followed by e, i, y, ä, or ö.
j is always pronounced like y, as in "yes".
k is pronounced somewhat, though not exactly, like sh, as in "ship" before e, i, y, ä, ö.
The letters *q, w, z* appear only in foreign words and some proper names. *q* becomes "k", *wa* "v", and *za* "s".
dj, gj, hj, lj are all pronounced like the English y
sch, sj, skj, stj are all pronounced like k.
sk is also pronounced as k, but only before e, i, y, ä, ö. Otherwise it is pronounced more like the English "scout" or "scare".
tj, kj are pronounced like the English sh in "shows".
ch is pronounced as the Swedish *tj/kj* before e, i, y, ä, ö, but pronounced as the sj/stj sound before a, o, å, u. (not common)
ng is usually one sound as in "singer" and "rang", and not like the English pronunciation of "finger".

And on a happy final note: *b, d, f, h, l, m, n, p, r, t, v, x* are pronounced and written as in English!

SURVIVAL PHRASES

english (Englishman/woman) **engelska (engelsk)**
Swedish **svenska**
England **England**
Sweden **Sverige**
Good morning! **god morgon!**
Good day/afternoon! **god dag!**
Good evening! **god kväll!**
Good night! **god natt!**
Goodbye **/Hej då!**
Do you speak English **talar ni engelska**
I don't understand. **jag förstår inte.**
Yes, that's right **ja (ha), jo, ju**
please! **var så god!**
thank you! **tack!**
thank you very much! **tack så mycket!**
Lady, Mrs **dam, kvinna**
Gentleman, Mr **herre**
(for) ladies **Damer**
(for) gentlemen **Herrar**
Where is…? **var är…?**
…Street **gatan**
  the road to… **vägen till…**
  the square **… platsen,…torget**
  the church **…kyrkan**
  the museum **museum, museet**
when? **när?**
open/opened **öppen/öppet**

town hall **stadshus**
post **postkontor**
stamp **frimärke**
bank **bank**
station **järnvägsstation**
hotel **hotell**
accommodation **övernattning**
How much is…? **vad kostar…?**
  a newspaper **tidning**
I would like… **jag skulle gärna…**
  a room **ha ett rum**
  a single room **med en bädd (enkelrum)**
  a double room **med två bäddar (dubbelrum)**
  with/without a bathroom **med bad / utan bad**
the key **nyckeln**
the toilet **toaletten**
a doctor **läkare, doktor**
right **till höger**
left **till vänster**
straight on **rakt fram**
above **uppe, ovanpå**
below **nedanför, nere**
new **ny**
expensive **dyr**
admission ticket **inträdesbiljett**

TRAFFIC SIGNS AND WARNINGS

Stop! **stopp! halt!**
Customs **tull**

Useful Words and Phrases

Caution! **se upp! giv akt!**
Slow! **sakta!**
Road works **vägarbete, gatuarbete**
One-way street **enkelriktad**
No through road! **genomfart förbjuden!**
Road closed **gatan avstängd**
Bathing forbidden! **badning förbjuden!**
No camping! **förbud mot tältning!**

MONTHS

January **januari**
February **februari**
March **mars**
April **april**
May **mai**
June **juni**

July **juli**
August **augusti**
September **september**
October **oktober**
November **november**
December **december**

WEEKDAYS

Monday **måndag**
Tuesday **tisdag**
Wednesday **onsdag**
Thursday **torsdag**
Friday **fredag**
Saturday **lördag**
Sunday **söndag**
Public holiday **helgdag**

NUMBERS

0	**noll**	10	**tio**	20	**tjugo**	80	**åttio**
1	**en, ett**	11	**elva**	21	**tjugoett**	90	**nittio**
2	**två**	12	**tolv**	22	**tjugotvå**	100	**hundra**
3	**tre**	13	**tretton**	23	**tjugotre**	101	**hundraen**
4	**fyra**	14	**fjorton**	25	**tjugofem**	200	**två hundra**
5	**fem**	15	**femton**	30	**trettio**	300	**tre hundra**
6	**sex**	16	**sexton**	40	**fyrtio**	725	**sju hundra tjugofem**
7	**sju**	17	**sjuton**	50	**femtio**	1,000	**tusen**
8	**åtta**	18	**arton**	60	**sextio**	1 million	**en million**
9	**nio**	19	**nitton**	70	**sjuttio**		

MENU READER

restaurang restaurant
kafeteria, barservering skinka ham
  cafeteria
gatukök takeaway
frukost breakfast
lunch, middag lunch
kvällsmat, middag
  dinner
äta eat
dricka drink
mycket, många much,
  many
lite little
räkning bill
betala pay
genast immediately
grillat grilled
stekt roast
kokt cooked, boiled
matsedel menu
soppa soup
kött meat
stekt roast, joint

korv sausage
skinka ham
älg elk
kcykling chicken
kalv veal
lamm lamb
ren reindeer/venison
oxe beef
gris pork
fisk fish
fiskbullar fish balls
torsk cod
forell, -laxöring trout
sill herring
räkor crab
lax salmon
rökt lax smoked
frukt fruit
äpple apple
apelsin orange
päron pear
jordgubbe
  strawberry

blåbär blueberry
hallon raspberry
körsbär cherry
plommon plum
lingon cranberries
citron lemon
grönsaker
  vegetables
blomkål cauliflower
böna beans
ärta peas
gurka cucumber
potatis potatoes
kål (rödkål) cabbage
  (red cabbage)
huvudsallat lettuce
spenat spinach
tomat tomato
dessert, efterrätt
  dessert
glass ice-cream
kompott compote,
  stewed fruit

sylt preserves
pudding pudding
vispgrädde Whipped
  cream
dryckor drinks
öl beer
kaffe coffee
mjölk milk
mineralvatten
  mineral water
grädde cream
te tea
vatten water
vin wine
vitvin White wine
rödvin Red wine
bröd bread
vetebröd white
  bread
franskt bröd roll
kaka cake
småkakor pastries
våfflor waffles

Street Atlas

For chapters: See inside front cover

Key to Road Atlas

	Public building, Building of interest	ℹ	Information
	Park	𝖬	Museum
	Pedestrian precinct	🎭	Theatre, opera house
—●—	Tramway/station	✟ ✡ ☪	Church / Synagogue / Mosque
—Ⓙ—	Railway (Pendeltåg)/station	📡 🯄	Television tower / Monument
—Ⓣ—	tube line (Tunnelbana)/station	★ ✡	Point of interest / Police
P ℙ	Parking area / multi-storey car park	✚ ✉	Hospital / Post office
		📖 ✳	Library / Scenic viewpoint
★	Top 10	⚠ Ⓒ	Youth hostel / Campground
26	Don't Miss	⚓ ⚒	Jetty / harbour
22	At Your Leisure	⌂ ⊨	Indoor swimming pool / Open air swimming pool

1 : 14.500

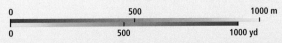

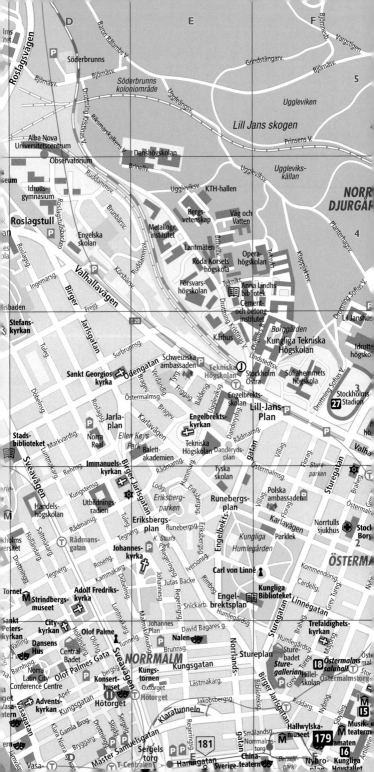

Street Index

Street Index

Index

A

ABBA The Museum 112–114
accommodation 38
airports, air travel 34, 171
alcohol 42
allsång 19–20
Antiquities, Gustav III's
   Museum of 82
Aquaria vattenmuseet (Aquaria
   Water Museum) 128
Aquaria Water Museum 128
Arkitektur- och designcentrum
   (Architecture Museum) 118
Armémuseet 63
Armoury 83
arrival 34, 171
art & crafts 72, 153
Artipelag 160

B

bars 74, 98, 136, 154
Beckholmen 111
Bergsgruvan 168
Bergsprängargränd 149
bike rental 37
Birger Jarl 14
Birger Jarls torn (Birger Jarl's
   Tower) 94
Birka 62
boat tours 23
Bondeska palatset (Bonde
   Palace) 94
Bonniers Konsthall 68
Brännkyrkagatan 167
bus services 36
Butterfly (and Bird) House 55

C

Carl XVI Gustaf, king 16
Changing of the Guard 84

children's activities 174
   ABBA The Museum 112
   Butterfly (and Bird) House 55
   Changing of the Guard 84
   Gröna Lund 127
   Junibacken 129
   Museum of Science and
      Technology 121
   Nature Recreation Area 143
   Prison Museum 143
   Rålambshovsparken 53
   SkyView 145
   Smedsuddsbade 53
   Tantobadet 168
   zoo 109
Christian II, king 14
cinemas 58
City Museum 140–141
city toll 12
climate & seasons 170, 174
clubs 74, 98, 136
Concessions 172
crispbread 32
currency 171
customs regulations 174
cycling 37, 164–165

D

Dansmuseet (Dance Museum)
   67
delicatessen 73
dental services 174
department stores 72
disability, travelling with a 174
Djurgården 99–130, 164–165
Dramaten 65
driving 37
Drottningholms Slott
   (Drottningholm Palace)
   158–159
Duke of Närke 115

E

East Asian Museum 126
eating out 70–71, 95–97,
   130
   beer garden 141, 149
Ehrenstrahl, David Klöcker
   92, 158
electricity 172
embassies 174
emergency telephone numbers
   173
entertainment 44, 74, 98, 130,
   153–154
Ericsson Globe 145
Estonia Monument 108
Etnografiska 121

F

Fängelsemuseume (Prison
   Museum) 143
fashion 73, 153
ferry services 36
festivals and events 18, 44,
   111
Finska kyrkan (Finnish Church)
   93
Fjärils- & Fågelhuset 55
food and drink 29–32, 42, 73,
   174
   see also eating out
   crispbread 32
   finger food 7
   gravad lax 30
   knäcka 32
   köttbullar 30
   smörgåsbord 29
   surströmmingh 30
foreign exchange 171
Fotografiska Museet
   (Museum of Photography)
   138–139

Index

Index

Picture Credits

Credits

1st Edition 2018

Worldwide Distribution: Marco Polo Travel Publishing Ltd
Pinewood, Chineham Business Park
Crockford Lane, Chineham
Basingstoke, Hampshire RG24 8AL, United Kingdom.
© MAIRDUMONT GmbH & Co. KG, Ostfildern

Authors: Rasso Knoller, Dr. Christian Nowak
Revised editing and translation: Sarah Trenker, Lietzow
Program supervisor: Birgit Borowski
Chief editor: Rainer Eisenschmid

Cartography: © MAIRDUMONT GmbH & Co. KG, Ostfildern
3D-illustrations: jangled nerves, Stuttgart

Printed in China

Despite all of our authors' thorough research, errors can creep in.
The publishers do not accept any liability for this. Whether you
want to praise us, alert us to errors or give us a personal tip –
please don't hesitate to email or post to:

MARCO POLO Travel Publishing Ltd
Pinewood, Chineham Business Park
Crockford Lane, Chineham
Basingstoke, Hampshire RG24 8AL
United Kingdom
Email: sales@marcopolouk.com

FSC
www.fsc.org
MIX
Paper from
responsible sources
FSC® C124385

10 REASONS
TO COME BACK AGAIN

1. The light **summer nights** are as fascinating as the clear **winter days**.

2. Some of the around **50 museums** have to be saved for a second visit.

3. On trips to the **skerries**, one keeps coming across new dream islands.

4. **Stockholm's restaurants** invite you to enjoy another culinary journey on your next trip.

5. Regardless of whether *allsång* or Midsummer – **great events** take place here all year round.

6. **Swedish designers** continuously produce surprises with their exciting creations.

7. You most certainly haven't discovered all the **walks and hikes** in and around Stockholm.

8. It is impossible to get tired of the **friendliness and helpfulness** of the Swedes.

9. The **palaces and palatial residences** turn every trip into a royal treat.

10. It is truly heavenly looking down on Stockholm from one of the many **viewing platforms.**